THESE ARE TH
LOO

MW00984474

"Rich with cautionary tales, lofty ideals, and unexpected heroes, pop culture's stories teach us in ways no lecture could. *Thy Geekdom Come* examines some of the most powerful and beloved narratives of geek culture and connects them to God's redemption story. This devotional delights the heart, stimulates the imagination, and edifies the soul."

ERIN STRAZA, MANAGING EDITOR
OF *CHRIST AND POP CULTURE* AND
AUTHOR OF *COMFORT DETOX*

"At last—a devotional that speaks to geeks! Not only can I relate to this devotional, I'm moved and inspired."

ALEX J. CAVANAUGH, AMAZON
BESTSELLING AUTHOR OF *CASSASTAR*

"*Thy Geekdom Come* challenges our perspective to help us love God and those around us in a deeper way. It's a great read with wonderful insights."

PAUL H. BOGE, AUTHOR OF *FATHER TO THE FATHERLESS*

"If we believe the redemption story found in the Bible is the greatest story ever told, we should expect to find echoes of it in pop culture. *Thy Geekdom Come* opens readers' eyes to how the geeky things they are already watching, reading, and playing relate to the good news Jesus came to announce."

DREW DIXON, CHIEF CONTENT NERD AT *LOVE THY NERD* AND EDITOR OF EXPLORE THE BIBLE: STUDENTS

"Brimming with enthusiasm for both Scripture and various corners of pop culture, *Thy Geekdom Come* offers encouraging, inventive ways to spend time with God's word. Who says morning devotions can't include a little *Mass Effect* and Miyazaki?"

JOSH LARSEN, EDITOR AND PODCAST HOST, *THINK CHRISTIAN*

"Faith is at its most vibrant when it's embodied in communities of imagination, and few people embody those qualities more than those within geek culture. *Thy Geekdom Come* brings this confluence together in a vibrant devotional resource for everyone. Blessed are the geeks!"

JAMIE ARPIN-RICCI, AUTHOR OF *VULNERABLE FAITH*

"*Thy Geekdom Come* is a rich trove of intelligent, surprising, pop-culture-infused meditations that take us from beloved imaginary worlds into the very heart of the gospel itself. In reading, I kept meeting friends old and new—characters, stories, and even whole universes that proved to be no mere object lessons, but genuine reflections of the beauty, truth, and goodness hard-coded into creation."

ADAM BRYANT MARSHALL, EDITOR

"This is a powerful work of Christian community. While the authors may not all technically live in the same neighbourhood, they occupy a very real social geography. Some authors wander down the familiar streets of movies, video games, and anime. Others prefer the back alleys and obscure corners of various geekdoms. Each find God already at work in these places. Brilliant!"

JARED SIEBERT, AUTHOR OF *GUTSY: (MIS)ADVENTURES IN CANADIAN CHURCH PLANTING* AND FOUNDER OF THE NEW LEAF NETWORK

THY GEEKDOM COME (VOL. 2)

42 SCIENCE FICTION-INSPIRED DEVOTIONALS

🦑 MYTHOS & INK

Cover art by Edreen Cielos (Paper Beats Rock)

ISBN 978-1-989423-28-8 (softcover), 978-1-989423-31-8 (ebook)

Published by Mythos & Ink
Winnipeg, Manitoba, Canada
www.mythosink.com

IN THE SERIES

Thy Geekdom Come: 42 Fandom-Inspired Devotionals

Thy Geekdom Come (Vol. 2): 42 Science Fiction-Inspired Devotionals

For all the science fiction fans who've been told they don't belong in church.

CONTENTS

Foreword   XV

1. THE IN-BETWEEN: DOCTOR WHO,   1
   HOPE, AND WAITING
   By Michael Penner

2. GOD OF ALL HNAU   7
   By Courtney Young

3. NO POWER IN THE 'VERSE CAN STOP   15
   FAITH
   By Jen Schlameuss and Jonathan Elsensohn

4. A LEAP THROUGH TIME IS NOT THE   21
   ANSWER
   By Charles Sadnick

5. FEZ AND THE FRACTAL DIMENSIONS   27
   OF FAITH
   By Aaron Thiessen

6. THIS IS THE WAY: DEVOTION LIKE THE   33
   MANDALORIAN'S
   By Ashley Mowers

7. CHRIST AS OUR MOCKINGJAY: 39
   GLUTTONY IN THE HUNGER GAMES
   By Allison Alexander

8. THE FAITH OF MOSES AND ADAMA   45
   By Robert White

9. COWBOY BEBOP, BELONGING,   51
   AND GOD
   By Kevin Cummings

10. SHADRACH, MESHACH, AND ABEDNEGO IN THE EMERGENCY INTELLIGENCE INCINERATOR
By Dan Bergman
57

11. THOR IS STILL WORTHY AND SO ARE YOU
By Jason Dueck
63

12. LIFE, DEATH, AND SCYTHE
By Dustin Schellenberg
69

13. EVERY RED SHIRT HAS A NAME
By Kyle Rudge
75

14. HOPE LIVES: SAMURAI JACK AND FINDING FREEDOM IN FORGIVENESS
By Allison Alexander
81

15. VIOLET EVERGARDEN AND THE PURPOSE OF PAIN
By Shaneen Thompson
87

16. METROID AND THE STATIONARY MOVEMENT OF GRACE
By Aaron Thiessen
93

17. THE GOOD PLACE AND IMPERFECT PEOPLE IN RELATIONSHIP
By Philippa Isom
99

18. A ROBOT'S FREE WILL
By Emma Skrumeda
107

19. POWER IN AKIRA AND THE CHURCH
By Justin Koop
113

20. GRACE IN STAR WARS: BATTLEFRONT II
By James Felix
119

21. BETRAYING THE DOCTOR AND JESUS
By Shaneen Thompson
125

22. THE THREE-BODY PROBLEM AND AN
    ERA OF CHAOS
    By Nathan Campbell   131

23. RAVEN AND THE TITAN OF FEAR
    By Jen Schlameuss   137

24. HUMANIZING ZOMBIES AND LEPERS
    By Allison Alexander   143

25. DIAL ME UP A 481
    By Philippa Isom   151

26. VOICES OF A NEARBY GOD
    By Charles Sadnick   157

27. A FLOWER IN THE SLUMS: JOY IN RUTH
    AND FINAL FANTASY VII
    By Victoria Grace Howell   163

28. REFLECTIONS OF IDENTITY IN 2001: A
    SPACE ODYSSEY
    By Nathan Campbell   169

29. THE VALUE OF CYBORGS AND
    SECOND-CLASS CITIZENS
    By Allison Alexander   175

30. WAR, PEACE, AND WONDERBEASTS
    By Kyle Rudge   181

31. CAST OUT THE SHADOWS: BAPTISM
    AND SHE-RA
    By Ashley Mowers   187

32. HEROES AND MISFITS: THE
    IMPORTANCE OF FAILURE IN
    OVERWATCH AND THE BIBLE
    By Dan Bergman   193

33. DOING GOOD IN AN UPSIDE-DOWN
    WORLD
    By Matt Civico   199

34. I SEE UNDEAD PEOPLE: THREE SPIRITUAL LESSONS FROM ZOMBIE APOCALYPSE FILMS
By Ellen Elliott
205

35. A VOICE FROM THE SKY: WONDER IN AN AGE OF SKEPTICISM
By Nathan Campbell
213

36. FINAL FANTASY VIII AND THE PROMISE THAT WE ARE NOT ALONE
By Lester Liao
219

37. A FATHER BY ANY OTHER NAME
By Emma Skrumeda
225

38. SOLOMON'S METHOD TO "LIVE LONG AND PROSPER"
By Robert White
233

39. FIGHTING THE GOOD FIGHT: CONFLICT IN THE GOSPELS AND ASIMOV'S FOUNDATION
By Tim Webster
239

40. TRUST, SURRENDER, AND DIRK GENTLY
By Jared and Nathan Siebert
245

41. FRINGE SCIENCE, IDENTITY, AND FREE WILL
By Allison Alexander
251

42. TALKING BACK TO THE TOTAL PERSPECTIVE VORTEX
By Emma Skrumeda
257

Acknowledgements
263

About the Writers
265

FOREWORD

After I was approached to write the foreword for this book, I started reading through the entries—beginning with excellent, thoughtful pieces on *I, Robot; The Avengers; Teen Titans;* and Star Wars—and I kept repeating the same phrase over and over to myself:

"Where was this book when I was younger?"

Growing up in the church as someone who loved comic books, video games, fantasy, and science fiction, I had a terrible time navigating the church's uneasy attitudes towards the things I loved. The messages I received tended to fall into two categories.

The first was the loud, often shrill, voice proclaiming that the books and movies I loved weren't "edifying" because they lacked explicitly Christian messages. I was told that Star Wars, Star Trek, X-Men comics, and other fandoms would only lead me from the path of the righteous and could jeopardize my eternal soul with their wickedness. The people who spoke with this voice were generally suspicious of imaginative things because the imaginative *suggests* and *points to* rather than clearly teaches. These people preferred instructive and overtly apologetic stories, ones they could be sure had the "right" messages. They "encouraged" me to read other (Christian) writers and usually had a long list of subpar but "safe" authors trying to replicate the sorts of stories I really enjoyed.

The other message I received—one that seemed pretty cool at the time but was actually deeply problematic—was that all the stories I liked were *really* about Jesus if you just read them the right way (and ignored most of the things that happened in them). This message was usually given by a well meaning youth leader or Sunday School teacher. They would take a film like *Star Wars* and would present it as Christian allegory, often ignoring key parts of the story or things that didn't support their limited interpretation.

"Luke Skywalker is just like Jesus," they would say. Or, "The Force is just like Jesus." Or, "Obi-Wan is just like Jesus." Something was always "just like Jesus."

As a total Star Wars geek, I frequently asked questions about how events or characters might impact their interpretation. I didn't mean it as a "gotcha" test to prove they weren't "real" fans, the way some try to police other fans; I was genuinely trying to engage someone I assumed was a geek for Star Wars like me. I usually left disappointed that my questions and observations were ignored or dismissed as unimportant to their specific Jesus-y reading. I quickly realized that their similes and metaphors didn't really respect the stories and characters I loved so much.

There are important spiritual and religious themes present in science fiction, fantasy, comic books, and television. Popular culture is fertile ground for conversations about belief, faith, God, and our place in the universe. I frequently teach university courses on the intersection between popular culture and religion, and these conversations—ones that Christians should be participating in—are happening all over the place. However, we need to respect and understand these texts rather than bend them to fit our frameworks. We need to engage honestly and humbly with these stories and the people who identify with these fandoms.

Science fiction and fantasy, in particular, need to be treated seriously, because people who like these genres *really* like them. You don't get many lukewarm fans of science fiction. I host a podcast called *Geek 4* that examines fans, fan cultures, and fan communities; whenever I interview science fiction or fantasy fans, I'm struck by how passionate they are—they go to conventions, cosplay, plan themed weddings, learn invented languages, and meet with other fans in person or online to discuss the minutiae of specific shows or movies.

The pieces in *Thy Geekdom Come* treat the source material and the people who love those worlds with respect. These writers are fans themselves, writing intelligently about the stories and franchises they love. There's no "shoehorning" the gospel where it doesn't fit. Instead, the authors draw connections and link between themes they find in beloved works (like *Doctor Who, 2001: A Space Odyssey,* and *iZombie*) and biblical themes. Each piece has an accompanying passage of Scripture as well as study questions to help the reader engage their minds. In these pages, you'll consider *Teen Titans* in relation to The Book of Wisdom, *Final Fantasy VII* and the promise in

Joshua that we are not alone. You'll reflect on the power of forgiveness in *Samurai Jack* and 1 Peter, and you'll read about imperfect people in *The Good Place* and 1 Thessalonians.

In drawing these connections and asking in-depth questions that go beyond the surface, the writers of *Thy Geekdom Come* invite us to engage the stories and characters we love in new, deeper, and exciting ways. It's the book I wish my younger self could have had.

Enjoy.

MICHAEL W. BOYCE, PHD, ASSOCIATE
PROFESSOR OF ENGLISH AND FILM
STUDIES AT BOOTH UNIVERSITY
COLLEGE

THE IN-BETWEEN: DOCTOR WHO, HOPE, AND WAITING

BY MICHAEL PENNER

"One more month and I'm free as the wind. Just look up there. Imagine you could go all the way out to the stars. That's where I'm going: into the sky, all the way up."

—Martha Jones, *Doctor Who*[1]

Read: Luke 23:50–56

Reflect: As we approached an Easter weekend without gatherings, I noticed some similarities between the COVID-19 pandemic and the disciples' experience after Good Friday. That Saturday—the Sabbath—was meant to be a day of rest. And though I'm sure the disciples refrained from working while sequestered, I cannot imagine their time was restful. Luke writes, "they rested according to the commandment."[2] I suspect taking it easy wasn't a top priority for them on that day.

Try to imagine: you've been following this leader for three years now. You were absolutely convinced that Jesus was the Chosen One. But when push came to shove, the Roman Empire was just too much, your leader didn't even put up a fight, and now he's dead. You are distraught. You are afraid for your life. You are trying to figure out how you could possibly go back to what you were doing before this whole thing started. To be sure, you have changed. You don't think you'll be the same person, even if you do go back to hauling fish into a boat every day. But today, you can do nothing. Today is the Sabbath, so you rest.

In the *Doctor Who* episode "Human Nature," the Doctor must become human in order to evade the detection of the Family, who are trying to consume his life energy to become immortal. He ends up hiding as a teacher in 1913 England. Martha, his companion, plays the part of a maid at the school, guarding his essence (and memories) as a Time Lord, which has been removed and stored in a pocket watch. Before the Doctor went through the transition, he left instructions for Martha: she is to bear the responsibility of hiding his secret until the time is right. As the teacher, the Doctor won't remember who he is or who Martha is. He won't remember their friendship.

Martha suffers alone while students mock the colour of her skin. The school nurse berates her for trying to help when the Doctor hits his head, saying "I daresay I know a lot more about [concussions] than you." The Doctor even fires her for insubordination. I admire her resolve as she fights the temptation to get the Doctor back before the time is right. In a particularly heart-wrenching scene, Martha reviews the Doctor's instructions, searching for something to help her, because he's falling in love with the school nurse. But this was a situation the Doctor had not foreseen, and she is on her own.

The time in between is challenging. Martha knows that she will soon be travelling the stars with the Doctor once more. But for now, she must be true to the responsibility given her.

The time in between requires wisdom. The disciples know that life must go on and that the Lord will deliver Israel somehow, sometime. But for now, they are left to grieve and process.

The time in between seems like it will last forever. Just as every illness has come and gone, there will be a day when COVID-19 is no longer a threat. But at the time of this writing, we have endured many months of it, and we are still called to maintain social distancing.

Waiting is never easy, but perseverance can produce faith and hope. At the end of Season Three, Martha faces an even more difficult challenge. The Master, another foe of the Doctor's, traps the Doctor, and it is up to Martha to save the world—an endeavor that requires patience and sacrifice. I'm not convinced she could have withstood this second "in between" had she not already born the despair of the first.

The disciples may have despaired on the Sabbath, but Jesus rose from the dead after three days. He didn't stay with them long after doing so, ascending to Heaven only 50 days later, and they were left to wait again. However, having learned to trust and believe the first time, their second waiting was in expectation more than fear.

We often look for a speedy end to waiting, suffering, and grieving—our time "in between." While we wait for COVID-19 to be over, or for employment, or for a diagnosis, or for news, or for help, we may be impatient. Who knows how the things we are learning in the midst of a pandemic will serve us in the future? For starters, I hope we will take our everyday maladies more seriously and do a better job of protecting people with compromised immune systems.

Looking for hope in these situations doesn't mean we aren't justified in anger at mistreatment, frustration at systems that exploit others, or grief at life's unfairness. But, perhaps, we can use the time to reflect on our divine calling. May we prepare to use the things we learn from those difficult times to make the world a better place once we emerge, taking our cold and lonely hallelujahs and turning them into more joyful songs.

Key Scripture

"[The disciples] asked him, 'Lord, is this the time when you will restore the kingdom to Israel?' He replied, 'It is not for you to know the times or periods that the Father has set by his own authority. But you will receive power when the Holy Spirit has come upon you; and you will be my witnesses in Jerusalem, in all Judea and Samaria, and to the ends of the earth.'" —Acts 1:6–8

Study Questions

1. Think of a time when you were waiting for something to happen. How were you tempted to speed up the process?

2. What lessons have you learned through waiting that have served you well afterward?

3. How does the time waiting for Jesus' return impact what you do in the here and now?

---

1. *Doctor Who.* "Human Nature," season 3, episode 8. Directed by Charlie Palmer. BBC Studios, 2007.
2. Luke 23:56

2

GOD OF ALL HNAU

BY COURTNEY YOUNG

"Two things about our world particularly stuck in their minds. ... The other was the fact that we had only one kind of *hnau*: they thought this must have far-reaching effects in the narrowing of sympathies and even of thought."

—Ransom, *Out of the Silent Planet* by C.S. Lewis[1]

Read: Job 39

Reflect: In *Out of the Silent Planet* by C.S. Lewis, a man named Ransom is abruptly transported to Mars (or, as its inhabitants call it, Malacandra). There, he finds himself a guest and an observer to a civilization very different from the one he left behind on Earth.

At the core of Malacandran civilization is the harmonious cooperation of multiple *hnau*, which is the word used to describe a sentient species. They are guided by a teacher and guardian named Oyarsa, a member of a celestial species, who intercedes between Creator and creation.

Unlike Earth, Malacandra does not have one sentient species, but three who live in on-going partnership. As Ransom is introduced to members of each species—the *hrossa, seroni,* and *pfifltriggi*—and learns something of their history and their customs, he comes to see how each views themselves as one part of a larger whole. At first, Ransom is suspicious of the genuine cooperation and mutuality between the *hnau* and tries to determine which *hnau* is master of the others to better ensure his continued survival.

As he questions and learns from his hosts, Ransom understands that, truly, each *hnau* values and stewards the gifts given to their people and, at the same time, values and is cared for by the talents of the others. They understand themselves to be siblings of their shared home. They are the interconnected progeny of one Creator and one ecosystem. As siblings, they know that each *hnau* has their own way of existing within and caring for their shared environment. Together, they are a chord in an unfolding cosmic tune.

Conversely, the *hnau* of Malacandra are fascinated by their guest, since Earth has been separated from its celestial neighbors for millennia. Earth's guardian had led the planet into depravity, and information from the silent planet had been cut off to protect the remaining planets. Ransom is humiliated when he compares the harmony of Malacandran society to the corruption on Earth.

"...[H]ow came it that the instincts of the *hrossa* so closely resembled the unattained ideals of that far-divided species [humans] whose instincts were so deplorably different?"

The Malacandrans are surprised to learn that humans are alone on Earth as the single sentient species. After talking with Ransom about life on Earth, they suspect that humans from Ransom's world lack empathy or reason, because they don't have other *hnau* to experience life with.

Because we aren't aware of any other sentient species in the universe, humanity thinks it's exceptional. And if a person or a society imagines themselves exceptional, then they have limited motivation to reach outside of their own experience or perception to seek wisdom. We are often motivated to force our will on everything around us because we believe we see everything clearly. This way of thinking is very different from the Malacandrans' philosophy, as they understand their life journeys to be inextricably bound together.

The Malacandrans' relationships with each other—the way they reach outside their own experiences to expand their perspective—reminds me of one of the most beautiful speeches in the Bible: God's response to Job's suffering in Job 38–41. Job has been in mourning after his life has fallen apart. Three friends come to comfort him and help him find meaning in what has happened. Their theologizing continually leads them back to the idea that Job must have sinned against God in some way and brought this suffering upon himself, but Job refuses to believe it.

Then, God speaks to Job. God does not offer a comfortable or clear explanation for Job's suffering.

Instead, God challenges Job to see the world from a different vantage point. God is not only Job's God, but also the God of rain and snow, goats and ostriches, hawks and horses, Behemoth and Leviathon. What does it mean that the God who was there when the foundations of the world were laid has come to speak to Job in his time of tragedy? The insight that Job gains from seeing his relationship with God from a different perspective seems to satisfy him, because he ends his period of mourning and begins to piece his life back together.

I wonder what Job took away from his conversation with God that helped him to re-engage with his life. Perhaps he was simply humbled, but when I read the text, I notice a new sense of belonging as a part of a whole. Job's suffering is not made meaningless because of God's largeness; indeed, this God, who could easily have ignored his pain to focus on the "bigger" picture, has not abandoned him. The God of oceans and bears has heard his every cry. Job begins to trust this God again, comforted by the all mighty being who has heard his cries.

Even given their peaceful ways, the *hnau* of Malacandra are not immune to tragedy. During his travels, Ransom sees that the civilization of the *hrossa*, *seroni*, and *pfifltriggi* used to be more prosperous, but is now dwindling. They admit their civilization is in decline and will die out some day, but together they do not fear it. They see it as a part of the ongoing process of creation and do not have any plans to resist their future.

I wonder how we humans would weigh the choices before us differently if we saw ourselves as siblings to all the other creatures of this planet and, at the same time, as creations of a God who celebrates the winters in Antarctica and the birds of the Amazon. If we saw trees as our companions, how much easier would it be to see the humanity in a stranger? If we saw ecosystems as something that produces us, how would that affect our business practices? What if humans are not the only *hnau* on this planet (or, indeed, the universe), but we have been too blinded by our own exceptionality to be able to see the creatures journeying through this life with us?

In the end, Ransom is given a choice to stay on Malacandra and live out his years in peace or to return to Earth on a dangerous voyage. Ransom chooses to go back—to humans, to depravity, to pain, and to hope. He determines:

> "Love of our own kind... is not the greatest of laws, but you, Oyarsa, have said it is a law. If I cannot live [on Earth], it is better for me not to live at all."

Like Job after his encounter with God, Ransom chooses to go home and begin a new life, one with a better sense for his place in the universe. His time with the *hnau* of Malacandra showed him that he belonged back on Earth where he could share the wisdom that had been shared with him by the *hrossa, seroni, pfifltriggi,* and Oyarsa about their shared Creator.

Ransom and Job both end up in painful, unexpected situations, as inevitably happens to all of us. They choose to listen and learn in the midst of their pain and confusion. They come to see that they are smaller than they thought they were, but their existence is held steady by so many more others from whom flow wisdom and strength, including our Creator God. While each has a humbling experience, they also see that they contain inherent value.

They are one note in the great unfolding opus of creation. Like Job and Ransom, in those moments when we feel alone or confused or hurt, we can listen for the wisdom and beauty that surrounds us and know that we are held in love by our Creator.

Key Scripture

> "In wisdom you have made them all; the earth is full of your creatures. Yonder is the sea, great and wide, creeping things innumerable are there, living things both small and great. There go the ships, and Leviathan that you formed to sport in it. These all look to you to give them their food in due season; when you give to them, they gather it up; when you open your hand, they are filled with good things. When you hide your face, they are dismayed; when you take away their breath, they die and return to their dust. When you send forth your spirit, they are created; and you renew the face of the ground." — Psalm 104: 24b–30

Study Questions

1. What are the other *hnau* on our planet that we can be living in relationship with?

2. When was a time that God invited, or challenged, you to widen your perspective? How did it change you?

3. What difference does it make to think of God as
God of the dinosaurs? God of neanderthals? God
of elephants? God of black holes? And God
of you?

---

1. Lewis, C.S. *Out of the Silent Planet*. John Lane, 1938.

NO POWER IN THE 'VERSE CAN STOP FAITH

BY JEN SCHLAMEUSS AND JONATHAN ELSENSOHN

"Only one thing is gonna walk you through this, Mal. Belief."

—Shepherd Book, *Serenity*[1]

Read: Romans 5:1–11

Reflect: If there's one feeling *Firefly* fans are intimately acquainted with, it's disappointment. There is a special cruelty in letting us get to know the loveable rogues of *Serenity*'s crew, invest in their plights, and care about what happens to them, just to have the show cancelled after its first season. The fans' perseverance was rewarded when, several years later, the film *Serenity* was released. In the spirit of all Joss Whedon projects, the movie brought some closure to the plot threads left dangling while killing off characters we cared about.

Disappointment and perseverance are at the heart of both the show and the film. From the very opening scene of the first episode, we see Captain Mal (then a sergeant in the Browncoats) holding an impossible position and trying to keep his weary troops together. They had been entrenched for weeks and are on the edge of defeat. But, Mal's leadership and faith keep them fighting for what they believe in. In a moment, though, all of that is crushed, as he learns that the promised reinforcements were never deployed. The Alliance is alone as troops overrun them with vastly superior numbers and equipment.

This defeat changes Mal. The faith that saw him through some of the darkest days of the war is gone. He has lost his trust in institutions, causes, humanity, and even God; he can't get past all that he has lost. So with his first mate, Zoe (the only other member of his battalion to survive the battle of Serenity Valley), he procures a Firefly class transport and aims to "just keep flying." He christens his new ship *Serenity*, a painful reminder of everything he left behind. In a deleted scene, we find out that Mal's choice to name his ship after his greatest defeat reflects his fixation with all he has lost. As Zoe explains in a deleted scene from the *Firefly*'s pilot, "Once you've been in Serenity, you never leave."

Along the way, Zoe and Mal pick up others who don't neatly fit the rigid, ordered universe the Alliance is striving to enforce. While they come from vastly different backgrounds, and even different planets, each member of the crew finds a home on *Serenity*. They come to care for one another as a family. Mal may not have been able to leave behind the pain of Serenity Valley, but the relationships he forges with his crew become the base of a new faith, replacing a portion of what was lost.

Some interesting interactions take place between Mal and Shepherd Book, a clergyman with a firm set of beliefs (and a mysterious past). While the two develop a strong bond, their outlooks on the universe could not be more different, at least as far as Mal sees it. Where the Shepherd counsels restraint, Mal is reactive. Where the Shepherd offers mercy, Mal seeks retribution. Despite their apparent differences, both men ground their sense of justice, morality, and responsibility in their abiding love for their fellow travellers.

When the Apostle Paul writes to the Romans about his understanding of the journey of faith, he doesn't describe his dramatic story of conversion. Not everyone will meet Christ on the road to Damascus. Instead, he draws the reader's attention to the struggles each of us find in the journey of faith, noting that suffering and endurance can lead to the development of hope when we're open to it (Romans 5:3–5). Challenges and setbacks do not diminish our faith, but provide us with a means of understanding God's presence in even the darkest parts of our lives.

After years of struggle and the deaths of several friends, Mal and the crew of the *Serenity* take refuge at the haven established by Shepherd Book. Mal confesses that he feels lost, uncertain of where to go and what to do. Book tells him that only belief will allow him to find his direction. When Mal bristles at the implication that God is the answer to his problems, Book redirects him to the significance of faith itself.

Mal's story is one of lost faith. As a man with a confused and violent past himself, Book realizes that Mal is not yet ready to perceive the presence of God in his life. The faith that Mal is able to understand is rooted in his crew—belief in love, respect, and shared sacrifice. The devastation he couldn't leave behind in Serenity Valley has been replaced by a tenacious faith in the family of his Firefly. Were it not for these bonds, the suffering he experienced could have destroyed him. But, because he endures, both he and the crew can transcend the trials that otherwise would swallow them.

Suffering that is not anchored by faith can destroy a person. Suffering when faith is present, even if that faith is as simple as the experience of community, can make people more resilient, hopeful, and compassionate. With God, suffering never has the last word. God created us for community so that we might bear one another's sufferings and lift one another up. For Mal, the truth of God's active presence in community may not ever be fully realized, yet he is able to experience it in the bonds of friendship and family.

The final scene of the movie shows Mal and the crew breaking through storm clouds, exiting the atmosphere to witness the sun rising above the planet. They had known so much loss, suffering, and death, but they were still together; they were still flying. While there was no shortage of disappointment, and things most certainly did not work out the way they would have chosen (or the fans may have wanted), their hope bloomed. The faith that God (whether they were able to recognize it or not) infused into their makeshift family made them able to overcome, together, any suffering that might come their way.

Key Scripture

> "I have said this to you, so that in me you may have
> peace. In the world you face persecution. But take
> courage; I have conquered the world!" —John
> 16:33

Study Questions

1. Has a major disappointment ever shaken your
faith? How did you overcome it?

2. In what ways has your community (however
you define it) helped to support you in a time of
trial?

3. How do you experience God when things don't
turn out the way you hoped? Do you get angry?
Do you turn away?

-----

1. *Serenity.* Directed by Joss Whedon. Universal Pictures, 2005.

4

A LEAP THROUGH TIME IS NOT THE ANSWER

BY CHARLES SADNICK

"Time waits for no one."
—Makoto, *The Girl Who Leapt Through Time*[1]

Read: Psalm 39

Reflect: A typical day in Makoto's life includes sleeping through her alarm, missing every question on a pop quiz, and setting her wok aflame during Home Economics. Clearly, she doesn't have everything together. In fact, she's exactly the type of person to lose control of her bike and tumble onto the path of a speeding train. Which she does. But then she's transported back in time a few minutes to right before the accident, and she is able to avoid the train.

For an awkward teen, there's no greater gift than time travel. A walking disaster no more, Makoto uses her powers to get perfect grades, make it to school on time, hit every baseball pitch, and relive a karaoke session. Life seems perfect, until she realizes that her actions can negatively impact others. She tries to fix problems her leaps have created and avoid undesirable situations, such as her friend Chiaki confessing his love to her, but she can't keep up.

I might not be able to comprehend time travel, but I understand making poor decisions when life gets frenzied. On the other hand, when life is going well—in time off, through financial gain, by other serendipitous means—I bask in the sun and idle away. I seem to only have two gears: moving too haphazardly or wasting time.

The Bible suggests life is too short to waste with either of these methods. David calls out in Psalms 39:4—"Lord, let me know my end, and what is the measure of my days; let me know how fleeting my life is." In the earlier verses of this passage, David talks about being filled with emotions and wanting to speak, but holding his tongue with his enemies. Then, he begs God for wisdom to understand how short his life is. David wants to be reminded that God is greater than he is and that his life is short in comparison to God's eternal nature. By saying, "let me know my end," he isn't requesting to know when he will die; rather, he wants to live a life that honours God with urgency.

David is a champion, a warrior, a king. He might not be able to travel through time, but he can topple giants with a slingshot and write poetry that will knock your socks off. It's easy to imagine him becoming arrogant (and, in later stories of the Bible, he does make some big, arrogant mistakes), but here he is humble. He compares people to "mere breaths" or in some translations, "a vapour." Humanity is fleeting compared to God, who is eternal. Therefore, we should think beyond our own lives, beyond gathering riches and going about "like a shadow."

In other words, David wants to live wisely and make each moment count.

For Makoto, that realization is almost too late. She tries to undo the mess she's created—a mess caused by focusing on frivolous changes to her life—but it's a challenging feat. She learns that a numbered tattoo on her arm is actually a countdown, showing how many leaps she has remaining. Eventually, she uses up all her leaps, leaving her helpless when two of her friends fall in front of a moving train just like she did at the beginning of the movie.

That's when Chiaki shows up. In a surprise reveal, he tells Makoto that the time leap device is actually his. He's from a distant future but has to use his own final leap to save their friends, meaning he is unable to stay in this time.

Makoto, who now realizes she's in love with Chiaki, is devastated. If she hadn't used her own time leaps on unimportant things, she could have saved their friends herself, and Chiaki could have stayed. Her wasted actions have dramatically changed the course of his life.

It's natural for us to live without thought of consequences, like Makoto, but what we do now matters. The prophets and apostles demonstrate, through both words and examples, that a faithful life is lived with urgency. (That doesn't mean we shouldn't rest, but that our actions should have purpose.) In Ephesians 5:15–16, Paul writes, "Be careful then how you live, not as unwise people but as wise, making the most of the time, because the days are evil." But what does "making the most of the time" even mean?

If I'm to take Christ's life as an example and consider

his greatest commandments,[2] perhaps it means putting others before ourselves. It must mean loving God with all our hearts, and relying on our Creator to reconcile us to our mistakes.

As Makoto grieves over what's she's done, she looks at her arm and notices that her tattoo has changed from zero to one. Chiaki had leaped to a point in time *before* Makoto used her final jump, restoring it to her and providing a final chance to make amends.

Like Makoto, I often make choices that leave things around me in shambles. The encouraging finale of *The Girl Who Leapt Through Time* reminds me that even when I make a mess of things, God can still redeem those mistakes. My errors are rarely the end of the tale.

As important as my past is, my future matters even more. As Makoto is reminded through words etched onto a chalkboard: "Time waits for no one." And that reminder is for us as well. It's time to get going.

Key Scripture

> "'Love the Lord your God with all your heart and with all your soul and with all your mind.' This is the first and greatest commandment. And the second is like it: 'Love your neighbor as yourself.'"
> —Matthew 22:37–39

Study Questions

1. Can you remember a time when you messed up

and God did something good with it anyway?
How did you learn from that experience?

2. Do you gear your actions towards having a "perfect" life instead of focusing on loving others?
What's one thing you can do to shift your perspective?

3. What does living "wisely," like Paul describes, look like?

---

1. *The Girl Who Leapt Through Time.* Directed by Mamoru Hosoda. Kadokawa Herald Pictures, 2006.

2. Matthew 22:37–39.

5

FEZ AND THE FRACTAL DIMENSIONS OF FAITH

BY AARON THIESSEN

"What's your favourite shape? Mine is square. Not cube, that's for sure! Because there is no such thing."
—Anonymous glasses guy in tutorial area, *Fez*[1]

Read: 1 Kings 19:1–15

Reflect: The basement looked like an Egyptian tomb, the walls papered with strange glyphs and symbols. Scrawled notes lay scattered across the floor. On the central screen, Gomez snored, asleep on the grass. And my friends and I were frantically chattering to one another, on the cusp of yet another discovery.

Though none of us were touching a controller, we were playing *Fez*—the indie puzzle-platformer from 2012.

Fez is unlike any other video game I've experienced. You, the player, take control of Gomez, a pixelated, 2D creature living life in his pixelated, 2D world. Quickly, however, you encounter a cosmic entity—a cube known as the Hexahedron. The cube gifts you with a magical fez, allowing you to see into the third dimension, but the cube also accidentally ruptures reality and is shattered across space.

On the surface, the game is straightforward. You must travel the world, tracking down the fragments of the Hexahedron. Mechanically, this is done by using the power of the fez to rotate the 2D world 90 degrees at a time, left or right along a vertical axis. The constant shifts in perspective invite you to create unintuitive paths between platforms to solve puzzles, reveal secrets, and collect the Hexahedron's cube fragments. As you collect items, your progress inches up to 100%, and many players are satisfied with stopping there.

However, if you're observant, you might notice strange patterns on a monument, bizarre symbols on a wall, or certain relationships between twinkling stars in the pixelated sky. None of these phenomena have obvious meanings at first. Are they merely decorative? Small windows into the game's lore? Something more?

Like donning a mystic fez from the cosmic beyond, players who stop to consider these mysteries will discover a whole new dimension to the game. The patterns, symbols, and relationships actually correspond to words, numbers, or directions. Following them leads to deeper puzzles: poems, riddles, secret messages, arcane artifacts. We thought we had finished the game, but these discoveries were swelling our completion percentage to 110... 150... 200%! How deep did these puzzles go?

This is what had so captivated my friends and me in my basement—the game had managed to press through the fourth wall and into our living space. Like peering at a fractal, the closer we looked at the game, the more complexity we found, its secrets itching the back of our minds.

That's the fascinating thing about *Fez*. While valuable as a simple puzzle-platformer, it also has this capacity to reach out of the screen, confront you in the here and now, and invite you to see the game differently... as long as you stop to notice and accept the invitation.

Oddly enough, there is something similar going on with Elijah in the Bible. On the surface, 1 Kings 19 is a fairly straightforward story. We have a deeply depressed Elijah, on the run in the wilderness, ready to give up on life because of the mess he finds himself in. An angel appears, feeds him, and Elijah continues to a mountain to speak with God.

Elijah waits for God in a howling wind, a violent earthquake, and a blazing fire, yet God's voice isn't found in a show of power, but rather in "a sound of sheer silence."[2]

There are straightforward meanings here that could take a lifetime to unpack: God does not abandon us in our wildernesses; God is not always to be heard in grand displays of power; God is present in the "sheer silences" of our lives. We might open ourselves to much truth here.

Yet—without diminishing any of those insights—if we take our time, look closer, and shift our perspective, additional meaning can reach out of the text and address us in a new way.

For example, an angel serving food is very unusual. In the Old Testament, there are stories of people serving angels, like Abraham and Lot, who entertain these divine messengers unawares. But this is the first time in the biblical narrative that we see an *angel* serving a *person*. Here, an angel approaches Elijah in his despondency, makes him a hot meal, and wakes him up to eat. And when Elijah is too depressed to do anything other than go back to bed, the angel allows him to do so!

Is this how we imagine God's demeanor toward us when we feel ground down and dejected? Certainly, God does not want us to wallow in sorrow but, here, God patiently addresses Elijah's practical needs before sending him onward. This is a new dimension of the text to explore.

Or how about this: did you notice that the text names at least four different modes through which God speaks to Elijah? There is, of course, the angel we just mentioned. But then there is the "word of the Lord" that comes to him in verse 9. And then this word is personified as a "he" in verse 11. What's going on there? Plus there's "a voice" that comes to Elijah from the sound of sheer silence. And finally there is the Lord speaking directly in verse 15.

God initiates communication with Elijah in many different ways, and Elijah picks up on each of them.

How can we open ourselves to hear God speak through the messengers, words, and voices that surround us everyday? Doing so requires active listening and careful discernment, and it seems God may be reaching out to us from unexpected places. Like in *Fez*, there is a new dimension here. To quote an anonymous ghost in *Fez*'s graveyard: "[Just] because you can't see something, doesn't mean it's not there."

Like the adventures of Gomez, a straightforward approach to scripture will get us places. Neither *Fez* nor the Bible require us to plumb every mystery to find satisfaction. But just as *Fez*'s completion rate can swell to over 200%, scripture is also supersaturated with meaning for those who embrace a surplus of perspective and who allow the Spirit to reach out through the text and address us directly. The tiny red hat is optional.

Key Scripture

> "...this grace was given to me to bring to the Gentiles the news of the boundless riches of Christ, and to make everyone see what is the plan of the mystery hidden for ages in God who created all things; so that through the church the wisdom of God in its rich variety might now be made known to the rulers and authorities in the heavenly places." —Ephesians 3:8–10

Reflection Questions

1. If you have the time, read 1 Kings 18, the story of Elijah's dramatic confrontation with the priests of Baal. In that climactic showdown, Elijah undeniably witnessed God's faithfulness in an all-consuming fire and the end of a crippling drought —a spiritual mountaintop experience. But here, just one chapter later, Elijah is cowering, depressed, and wishes for death. What do you think caused Elijah to crash so hard in chapter 19? Does this change the meaning of the angel's patient care for him? Have you ever experienced such a spiritual mood swing?

2. Elijah was attuned to God's communication from a number of different sources. Where do you find yourself expecting to hear from God? Where might you open yourself to a surprise address?

3. Richard Rohr once said that "[God's] mystery is not something you *can't* know. [God's] mystery is *endless knowability.*"[3] Do you agree? As we reflect on the supersaturated nature of scripture, are there any limits we must keep in mind?

---

1.   *Fez.* Microsoft Windows, Polytron Corporation, 2013.

2.   1 King 19:12.

3.   Rohr, Richard. "Mystery is Endless Knowability." Center for Action and Contemplation. August 23, 2016, https://cac.org/mystery-endless-knowability-2016-08-23/.

6

THIS IS THE WAY: DEVOTION LIKE THE MANDALORIAN'S

BY ASHLEY MOWERS

"A foundling is in your care. By creed, until it is of age or reunited with its own kind, you are as its father. This is the Way."

—The Armourer, *The Mandalorian*[1]

Read: Matthew 5

Reflect: There's a joke that goes around seminaries: "There's a reason 'seminary' and 'cemetery' sound so similar." At my time of study, the quip referenced our exhaustion due to the remaining papers and chapters we had to complete before the end of term. Now I consider the tongue-in-cheek remark with more warmth and appreciation, as I relate it to a sense of death to self.

In the New Testament theology class I took during my final term, we reflected on the Beatitudes in Matthew 5 during each session. The professor pushed us to reconsider our self-perception, saying, "We like to think of ourselves as among the blessed listed here. Are we really?"

We may think of ourselves as meek, hungering and thirsting for righteousness, merciful, pure in heart, or peacemakers, but are we taking any actions to reflect these beatitudes in our daily lives?

The Beatitudes are connected to another famous speech by Jesus:

> "'You shall love the Lord your God with all your heart, and with all your soul, and with all your mind.' This is the greatest and first commandment. And a second is like it: 'You shall love your neighbor as yourself.' On these two commandments hang all the law and the prophets."[2]

At the beginning of each class, we would recite this creed and at the end, we'd pray the Lord's Prayer. Nearly every class, we were asked, "Who is your neighbour?" and "Are you included in the Beatitudes?" For those unused to repetition in their worship services, this may seem redundant, but it started to shape the way we saw and interacted with the world. By the end of the term, we began to decenter our identities and needs in exchange for those of the people in immediate proximity to us. Constantly thinking about these scriptures encouraged us to act upon them.

The Armourer quickly became one of my favourite characters in *The Mandalorian* for several reasons. First, I find her anonymity, much like the Mandalorian's, intriguing and empowering; her gear is pragmatic and understated, plus she's a seasoned warrior. Second, she exhibits discipline and self-restraint. Despite the demonstration of her combat skill by the end of the first season, she only uses her abilities when life is threatened. Finally, her knowledge of and devotion to the Mandalorian Creed and its history are most impressive, and her mentorship of the Mandalorian looks much like the relationship between a priest and her parishioners, or Christ and his disciples.

She is certainly devoted to the Way of the Mandalore. In Season One, Episode Eight, "Redemption," she rejects the Mandalorian's invitation to escape with him, stating, "I will not abandon this place until I have salvaged what remains." On its surface, this could be seen merely as a dedication to the tradition of forging armour and weaponry for the Mandalorians. However, the Way is much more than piecing together the history and legacy of a warrior. Not only has she taken in foundlings, but she insists on the care and protection of one who demonstrates the qualities of their historic enemy, the Jedi. By all rights, she should hate what the Child, a Force-sensitive youngling who looks like a miniature Yoda, represents— the return of Force-wielding beings.

But the Child's potential enmity does not keep the Armourer from following the Creed; instead, Baby Yoda reveals the fullness of it. "A foundling is in your care. The Creed: until it is of age, or reunited with its own kind, you are as its father. This is the Way." This sounds an awful lot like what follows the Beatitudes in Matthew 5:43–48:

> "You have heard that it was said, 'You shall love your neighbor and hate your enemy.' But I say to you, love your enemies and pray for those who persecute you, so that you may be children of your Father in heaven; for he makes his sun rise on the evil and on the good, and sends rain on the righteous and on the unrighteous."

To the Armourer, it doesn't matter whether the Child could grow into a potential enemy. What matters is that it's an orphan, it's vulnerable, and they can help it. The Armourer refocuses the narrative of her own tradition from herself to the Child. In doing so, she serves the least of these, not only maintaining commitment to her religion, but revealing its depth. She protects the Child by claiming it's one of their own, making the youngling and the Mandalorian a clan of two, complete with their own signet (a mudhorn).

Earlier in the series, it was briefly mentioned that signets were revealed, rather than chosen. This signet was not fully revealed until the Mandalorian was charged with care of the Child, thus creating his own clan. This symbol is not merely a demonstration of commitment, but a fulfilment and great commission as she sends her mentee on with this charge.

The emergence of this clan is compelling, as so much of the Child's past and future are still a mystery. The baby could still grow to be a great threat to the Way of the Mandalore. By this brave decision, the Armourer demonstrates a faith in and devotion to the Way beyond a dependency on evidence and assurances. She extends the covenantal practices of her discipline to a (seemingly) helpless being who can offer them nothing in return. And because the Mandalorian is a faithful pupil, he accepts this new role without complaint.

I hope I grow into faith this strong, even though that very strength terrifies me. Life is, in many ways, much easier when I get to be the Child. It's a lot harder when I'm in the position of the Armourer or the Mandalorian, risking what little remains of my station and tradition. I may be tasked with sticking my neck out with no gratification whatsoever. Some days, extending a hand to the hopeless and helpless is exhausting. So many need help. What if something bad happens? What if I run out of resources? What if nothing changes? But in Matthew 5, Christ isn't addressing concerns of insufficiency, he's describing the character of the Kingdom to come. If I can help mirror that Kingdom, even in a small way, I will.

Blessed are the orphans, for they shall be adopted. Blessed are the abandoned, for they shall be given a tribe. Blessed are those who care for the least of these, for they have served the Lord. Blessed are those who have nothing, for they shall be given *everything*.

This is the Way.

Key Scripture

> "Religion that is pure and undefiled before God, the Father, is this: to care for orphans and widows in their distress, and to keep oneself unstained by the world." —James 1:27

Study Questions

> 1. What are some things that might keep you from seeing yourself in the Beatitudes in Matthew 5 and acting out Christ's instructions to love each other? These could be external (e.g. time, health) or internal (e.g. fear, laziness). What's something, however large or small, you can do to overcome those obstacles and love your neighbour today?

2. Reflect on the Beatitudes and the ways God provides for you. How can you say thank you?

3. How can you love your "enemy" today? Pray for someone you dislike, who has treated you unfairly, or who your culture tells you isn't invited into your family (perhaps because of a "taboo" sin or behaviour). Try practicing this whenever you pray and see if it impacts your behaviour towards those people.

---

1. *The Mandalorian.* "Chapter 8: Redemption," season 1, episode 8. Directed by Taika Waititi. Disney, 2019.
2. Matthew 22:37–40.

7

CHRIST AS OUR MOCKINGJAY: GLUTTONY IN THE HUNGER GAMES

BY ALLISON ALEXANDER

"Peeta looks at the glass ... 'You mean this will make me puke?' My prep team laughs hysterically. 'Of course, so you can keep eating,' says Octavia. 'I've been in there twice already. Everyone does it, or else how would you have any fun at a feast?'"
—*Catching Fire* by Suzanne Collins [1]

Read: 2 Samuel 11–12:14

Reflect: In the society of the Hunger Games series, people are controlled by poverty and oppression. Katniss comes from the poorest area, District 12, and regularly breaks the law by hunting and selling game on the black market so her family can survive. It's no surprise that she's appalled at the Capitol citizens' privilege. When she first visits the Capitol in *The Hunger Games*, she learns that the people there aren't starving; they have all their physical needs taken care of and are more concerned with physical and social appearances than anything else.

After winning the Games in the first book, Katniss and Peeta are rewarded in the second with riches, parties, and more food than they can eat. The sheer amount of tasty treats at a Capitol feast overwhelms them. Determined to sample everything, Katniss fills up quickly even though she's only taking one bite of each dish. When people from the Capitol ask her why she's stopped eating, she says, "I can't hold another bite," and they laugh.

> "They lead us over to a table that holds tiny stemmed wine glasses filled with clear liquid. 'Drink this!'
>
> Peeta picks one up to take a sip and they lose it.
>
> 'Not here!' shrieks Octavia.
>
> 'You have to do it in there,' says Venia, pointing to doors that lead to the toilets. 'Or you'll get it all over the floor!'"

The Capitol's citizens indulge in everything, and doing so harms other people. The citizens of other districts are being mistreated, are working under horrible conditions, are starving, are dying, and the Capitol hoards resources and is the direct cause of their suffering. The majority of the Capitol's citizens have been enculturated into behaving this way and believing that gluttony is the only way of life. That doesn't excuse their actions or the people they are oppressing, but speaks to the difficulty of overthrowing a system that's designed to oppress others.

Gluttony is often defined as overeating, but it is not necessarily about food, and it is certainly not about being fat. I appreciate how Amanda Martinez Beck, author of *Lovely: How I Learned to Embrace the Body God Gave Me*, defines it:

"Gluttony isn't eating too many pizza slices. Gluttony is engaging in consumption—not restricted to food—that harms our neighbor. Think of our consumer culture and consider what that might include ... affordable housing made unattainable by gentrification (overconsumption of location)? Predatory payday lending (overconsumption of profit)? Disenfranchisement of poor people through changing political districts (overconsumption of power)?"[2]

The people of the Capitol are gluttons because they have access to food, wealth, housing, safety, training, and clothing, and they deny others similar privileges. Their misuse of power reminds me of David in the Bible—not the boy who brought down Goliath with a rock and a slingshot, but the grown-up king who has realized he can have whatever he wants. Adult David has changed much since his time as a shepherd.

David does something horrific in 2 Samuel 11—one day, when he's walking on his roof, he sees a woman, Bathsheba, taking a bath and thinks she's beautiful. He finds out she's someone else's wife, but orders her brought to him anyway. Later, when she becomes pregnant, he has her husband killed to cover up his own sin.

In the next chapter, God sends the prophet Nathan to David. Nathan tells David a story about a rich man, who has many herds, and a poor man, who has only one lamb. The rich man takes the poor man's lamb—all that this man has and loves—and slaughters it for a meal when he could have used one of his own animals.

David is outraged at this story and ready to punish the "rich man" that Nathan is talking about. But, of course, the story is about him. *He* is the rich man, and God is angry at David for being selfish. David abuses his power, wanting someone else's wife when he already has many and trying to hide his wrongdoing by killing an innocent man who was loyal to him.

David's sin is taking something that is not his and exploiting his power. God forgives David when he acknowledges what he did was wrong, but David still has to deal with the consequences of his actions.

Acknowledging we're wrong is a first step towards healing and reconciliation, but sometimes that recognition is a process in itself.

In *Catching Fire*, Katniss doesn't bother trying to explain to her prep team how they're privileged, because she knows they wouldn't understand. They would just brush her aside because this is all that they know, and words aren't enough to convince them to look outside their selfish lives. It's not until Katniss almost dies and their society crumbles around them that they even begin to comprehend their privilege.

Others, like Haymitch and Peeta, immediately understand Katniss's hatred of the Capitol, because they are from District 12 themselves and have lived in poverty. Then there are people like Katniss's stylist, Cinna; he seems to have come from a privileged background, but he uses his station to help Katniss. Cinna designs beautiful clothes, things that could be considered frivolous, yet he uses his talents to assist Katniss in the Games, to give her courage, to help her become a symbol for the rebellion.

Recognizing our own gluttony means looking at how we, as individuals and as a society, engage in consumption that harms our neighbours. Then we ask for forgiveness and try to do better. The cross is our symbol of rebellion, for Jesus came to free the oppressed and we model ourselves after him. Often, like David, our pride gets in the way and we hurt others. Our mistakes don't mean we shouldn't continue to try to be better; for Christ is our example, and he lifts up the oppressed.

Key Scripture

"The Spirit of the Lord is upon me, because he has anointed me to bring good news to the poor. He has sent me to proclaim release to the captives and recovery of sight to the blind, to let the oppressed go free." —Luke 4:18

Study Questions

1. Name three ways our society perpetuates gluttony and consider what steps of action you can take to stop it.

2. Why was David surprised to learn he was the "rich man" in Nathan's story? How do we become blind to our own gluttony?

3. What are areas of life where you are privileged, and how can you use your advantage to help others who lack those privileges?

1. Collins, Suzanne. *Catching Fire*. Scholastic, 2009.
2. Beck, Amanda Martinez. "Is Gluttony a Sin?" *Fat In Church Issue* 3. May 2019, https://tinyletter.com/FatinChurch/letters/issue-3-is-gluttony-a-sin.

8

THE FAITH OF MOSES AND ADAMA

BY ROBERT WHITE

"Fleeing from the Cylon Tyranny, the last battlestar, *Galactica*, leads a ragtag fugitive fleet on a lonely quest... a shining planet known as Earth."
—Commander Adama, *Battlestar Galactica* (1978 series), Opening Credits[1]

Read: Exodus 16:1–12

Reflect: In the opening of the original *Battlestar Galactica* TV series, representatives of the Twelve Colonies meet with delegates from the Cylon Empire to celebrate a peace treaty. In true science fiction fashion, the Cylons—robots created by an alien race—want anything but peace.

The meeting proves to be a ruse. Helped by the traitorous human Baltar, hidden Cylon forces appear, attack, and annihilate almost everyone on the human planets. The Twelve Colonies' forces are decimated, including every battleship but the battlestar *Galactica*. Survivors escape in a variety of ships, from cargo ships to scientific exploration vehicles, and rendezvous with the *Galactica*. When representatives of the 220 ships meet, Adama—the commander of the *Galactica*—tells them that their survival depends on leaving their galaxy and finding a mythical thirteenth colony that settled on a distant planet known as Earth.

Re-watching this series as an adult, I noticed that the special effects were dated, the acting could have been better, and the plots were more formulaic than I remembered. Airing for only one season, each episode begins with either a crisis—such as a lack of food—or a crew member hearing about someone who knows something about Earth. The Cylons always arrive to stop the *Galactica* from obtaining what they need. A battle ensues. The Cylons lose. The humans end up with what they need in order to continue their quest. Each episode ends with Adama's sonorous tones expressing his faith that eventually his people will find the "shining planet known as Earth."

Described by series' creator Glen A. Larson as "a little like the Exodus,"[2] *Battlestar Galactica* depicts a journey similar to the biblical story of the Israelites' journey from Egypt to the promised land of Canaan. Almost from the beginning, both Commander Adama (the leader of *Galactica*'s convoy) and Moses (God's chosen leader of the Israelites) face challenges.

While fleeing from the Cylons, the *Galactica* comes across a void, which blocks their escape route. As Adama considers his options, he increasingly believes the *Galactica* must cross the void, and says so to his second-in-command, Colonel Tigh:

Adama: "The Book of the Word tells us that a great star guided the Lords of Kobol away from the dying planet, across an endless black sea."

Tigh: "The void? Adama, there are probably as many voids in the universe as there are ideas."

Adama: "Can we turn our backs on the inspiration that delivered our people once before?"[3]

The *Galactica* crosses the void and finds a planet that the thirteenth tribe stopped at on its way to Earth. While exploring a tomb for more clues, Baltar questions Adama's belief in the distant planet.

Baltar: "Adama, listen to reason. You could drift forever in search of what? A planet that may be the myth of half drunken star voyagers who came back to die here?"

Adama: "Our safety is not behind us with you or the Cylons. It lies somewhere out there along the path taken by the thirteenth tribe, the tribe that colonized the planet Earth."

Baltar: "You can't be serious. That's nothing but a fable."

Adama: "I believe it is as real as the existence of the thirteenth tribe."[4]

This isn't the only time Adama's faith is questioned. But in each episode, when all seems lost, either his knowledge of the Book of the Word or an incident reaffirms his faith in the legend of Earth and strengthens his beliefs.

Unlike the survivors of the Cylon attack, the Israelites

have proof that Moses is following God's lead: they witness miracles like the plagues and the parting of the Red Sea. Throughout their journey, every time they complain about their lack of resources, Moses prays and God provides. Even when Moses doubts, like the time he tells God, "I am not able to carry all these people alone, for they are too heavy for me,"[5] God says seventy of Israel's elders will be equipped to help Moses share the burden of the people.

Yet, doubt continues to run rampant throughout the Israelites. When they are about to enter Canaan, the people balk. Moses sends twelve men, one from each tribe, to spy out the land. When they return, they tell of a plentiful land that is filled with fortified towns and strong warriors. Ten of the spies think the Israelites are no match for the people of Canaan, while two, Joshua and Caleb, believe the Israelites can win.

The Israelites side with the ten, wondering why Moses led them from oppression in Egypt to death in Canaan. They decide they should choose a new leader and return to Egypt. When God threatens to destroy them with a plague, Moses intercedes and asks God to forgive them. God does, but declares no one from that generation, except Caleb and Joshua, will enter Canaan.

The writer of the book of Hebrews describes faith as hope in things unseen. For both Adama and Moses, this means the journey is less important than the belief in the final destination. Moses also has faith in the One who is by his side on the journey. Adama's steadfast faith rewards him when the band of ragtag fugitives finally finds Earth (in a sequel series aired in 1980). Moses' faith leads the

Israelites to the Promised Land, but only after forty years of wandering in the desert.

Our journey may have as many twists and turns as those of the *Galactica* or the Israelites, such as financial setbacks, family crises, health challenges, or fractured relationships. There are times when the phrase "take joy in the journey" rings as hollow as the void Adama crossed. There are times when doubt makes the journey seem as bleak as the desert the Israelites wandered in for a generation. While faith may not change our circumstances, we can find hope in believing good lies at the end and in the God who journeys with us.

Key Scripture

> "Now faith is the assurance of things hoped for,
> the conviction of things not seen." —Hebrews 11:1

Reflection Questions

1. Why do you think the other ten spies were afraid, even when they'd seen signs of God's power? When have you experienced that kind of fear?

2. The writer of Hebrews describes faith as an assurance of and conviction in things you hope for but don't see. How has faith played out in your spiritual journey?

3. Where are you in your journey: the void, the

desert, somewhere else? Is your faith in the
journey or in the end of the journey?

———————————————————

1. *Battlestar Galactica.* Season 1. Directed by Richard A. Colla et. al.
   NBC Universal, 1978–1979.
2. *Battlestar Galactica* DVD box set. "Interview with Glen A. Larson."
   Universal Studios, 2004.
3. *Battlestar Galactica.* "Lost Planet of the Gods: Part 2," season 1,
   episode 3. Directed by Christian I. Nyby. NBCUniversal, 1978.
4. *Battlestar Galactica.* "Lost Planet of the Gods: Part 2."
5. Numbers 11:14

9

COWBOY BEBOP, BELONGING, AND GOD

BY KEVIN CUMMINGS

"It's the best. Belonging is the very best thing there is."
—Faye Valentine, *Cowboy Bebop*[1]

Read: Luke 15

Reflect: Faye Valentine and Radical Ed just want to find their way home. For Faye, this means connecting with a past she can't remember due to amnesia. For Ed, it means finding the father who had abandoned her in an orphanage. Neither of them know that their quests will turn out quite different from what they imagine.

Faye's problem is largely temporal. Before going to space, she lives a life of privilege on Earth with loving parents. An accident on a spaceship kills them and leaves her seriously injured. She's placed in cryostasis until she can be healed—a process that leaves her physically fit but completely unable to remember her childhood. Betrayed by the people who are supposed to help her, Faye survives by turning to cynicism and petty crime. It is a poor alternative to what she could have become, but it is the best she can do under the circumstances.

In a word, Faye is lost.

Radical Ed (Edward Wong Hau Pepelu Tivruski IV), the teenage genius hacker on the *Bebop*, is lost as well. In Ed's case, however, the term *abandoned* might be more accurate. Ed is left at a daycare and forgotten by her work-obsessed father. She wanders into an orphanage and stays for a while before leaving to find her way in the world. Learning about the *Bebop,* she engineers a way to become part of the crew. For a while, that scratches her itch to belong. Eventually, restlessness sets in and she feels driven to find her way home.

The New Testament often explores the idea of lost-ness. In the book of Luke, Jesus is challenged by religious leaders for dining with sinners and tax collectors. In response, Jesus tells three stories about lost things: a lost sheep, a lost coin, and a lost son.

In the parable of the lost sheep, the shepherd goes into the wilderness on a quest to reclaim what was lost to him. Likewise, the woman who loses a coin (one tenth of her total wealth) lights a lamp, sweeps the house, and searches carefully. Ed wants to be like that sheep and coin—valued and treasured.

Instead, Ed has to seek out her absent father. Applying her hacking skills, she puts out a fake bounty on him. When the crew of the *Bebop* finds him, he greets Ed with excitement and thanks the *Bebop* crew for returning his child to him. Unfortunately, ever work-obsessed, he runs off again mere minutes after the reunion. By his actions, Ed's father makes it clear that Ed isn't a priority.

At the end of the parable of the lost son, the son

chooses to return to his homeland with the intent of becoming a servant. He heads for his father's house, ashamed of his failure. Perhaps he could have chosen to go elsewhere to be a servant, and surely it would have been less embarrassing, but he chooses to return to his family. He wants to belong.

Which brings us back to Faye. Mid-way through the series we get a glimpse of her as a child in a video tape that is delivered to the *Bebop*. On the tape, she is young, outgoing, and enthusiastic. She is nothing like the cynical, self-centred Faye we know. Confused, she watches her younger self enthuse, "And now a big cheer from my heart. Let's... go... me, all right! Do your best! Do your best! Don't lose, me!"[2]

From the moment she is revived, Faye is betrayed over and over by those who are supposed to be helping her. She lives by a philosophy of "leave before being abandoned" and struggles to trust her shipmates. Underneath it all, though, is a drive to get back to the only real home she has known. Like the lost son, Faye wants to return home.

Faye eventually returns to Earth and goes to the place she saw on the video. She encounters an old woman who had been one of her childhood friends, and this meeting triggers a flood of memories. For the first time since being revived, Faye feels like she has found a place to belong. Excited, she heads off in her ship to return to the home she lost. As she departs, she tells Ed that belonging is the best thing there is.

The older brother in the parable doesn't feel like his lost brother deserves that kind of belonging. Hearing that his sibling has returned, he refuses to join in the party and reminds his father of the younger son's sins. To put it succinctly, he "others" his own sibling. He denies that his brother belongs in the family.

The younger is not the only brother who is "lost" in this story.

The parables in Luke 15 are designed to accomplish two things. First, they give us comfort in the knowledge that God is always looking for us. Second, they encourage us to confront our judgement of others. Remember that the chapter starts with the challenge from the religious leaders; they are incensed that Jesus is hanging out with the "wrong" kind of people.

As geeks, it's easy to feel like outsiders. The larger world doesn't understand—often doesn't *want* to understand—our interests and obsessions. It's easy to feel like we're facing a hostile land.

It's also easy to judge others. Have you ever said or heard anything like the following?

- "You can't call yourself a *true* Star Wars fan if you liked *The Last Jedi*."
- "You can't really love anime unless you've slogged through all the original *Pokémon* episodes."
- "You're not a real gamer unless you play hardcore shooters."

Anytime we assert that our fandom is better or (worse yet) that we are a "true" fan, we've moved out of the place of love and openness into judgement. Being judgmental can become a habit. Before long, we find ourselves evaluating everyone to determine whether they are part of our preferred circle. This process is called "othering," and it is exactly the kind of thing that Jesus is warning against in Luke chapter 15.

The parable of the lost son ends with the father encouraging the elder son to join the celebration. Jesus leaves the story unresolved, inviting us to consider how we resemble the older brother. As believers, we are called to show God's love to the world. This means loving everyone whether or not we think they belong.

Faye was on to something when she said that belonging is the best thing there is. As followers of Christ, we are challenged to offer the experience of "belonging" to everyone.

Key Scripture

"You shall not oppress a resident alien; you know the heart of an alien, for you were aliens in the land of Egypt." —Exodus 23:9

Study Questions

1. Have you ever felt like Ed, like you've wanted to be the lost sheep or coin—loved, valued, and searched for? How can you help someone else feel valued in that way?

2. Have you ever felt like Faye with a "leave before you're abandoned" mentality, even though you wanted to belong? What's a step you can take to learn how to trust others?

3. Have you ever felt that you were being "othered" for something that was important to you? Have you ever "othered" someone else? How do the parables encourage you to respond in the future?

---

1. *Cowboy Bebop.* "Hard Luck Woman," session 24. Directed by Hiroki Kanno. Adult Swim, 1999.
2. *Cowboy Bebop.* "Speak Like A Child," session 18. Directed by Hiroki Kanno. Adult Swim, 1999.

10

SHADRACH, MESHACH, AND ABEDNEGO IN THE EMERGENCY INTELLIGENCE INCINERATOR

BY DAN BERGMAN

"Fantastic. You remained resolute and resourceful in an atmosphere of extreme pessimism."
—GLaDOS, *Portal*[1]

Read: Daniel 3

Reflect: At first glance, *Portal* is a game about exploring the physics made possible by the Aperture Science Handheld Portal Device, more commonly known as the Portal Gun. You (as the resourceful protagonist, Chell) make your way through several test chambers, solving puzzles which have been carefully designed by the facility's scientists.

Along the way, however, you become suspicious of the true nature of the lab and the experiments. You notice that there are no other humans in the facility. The only intelligent being you can interact with is the guiding, disembodied, robotic voice of GLaDOS (Genetic Lifeform and Disk Operating System). As the game goes on, her tone becomes more insincere, more passive-aggressive. She "guides" you through more and more dangerous tests, involving machine gun-toting robotic sentries, acidic pits, and lethal orbs of energy. You discover hidden rooms with the scrawlings of test-subjects past, which confirms your suspicion that the cake GLaDOS has been promising on completion of your trials is, in fact, a lie. You realize that GLaDOS doesn't want you to succeed.

At the end of the "final" test chamber, GLaDOS reveals that you are no longer necessary as part of the experiment. You are slowly lowered into the Emergency Intelligence Incinerator, with no apparent way out. To GLaDOS's chagrin, your resourcefulness, gained from completing a series of complex challenges with your Portal Gun, allows you to find a way out of the Incinerator. You find a network of hallways unintended for test subjects to discover. Then, you incinerate GLaDOS and escape to the surface.

It turns out that Aperture Science, which was once a thriving science lab, had been taken over by GLaDOS years prior when she used a neurotoxin to kill all the scientists inside. In all that time, her drive to test subjects had not disappeared. The facility that was supposed to bring about a utopian scientific tomorrow had been turned into a sick dystopian playground for the evil Operating System to mess with its human subjects—until Chell put a stop to it!

We read about a different dystopian reality in the biblical book of Daniel (a phenomenal book title, if you ask me). Like *Portal*, this story has a narcissistic ruler and an incinerator.

After hundreds of years making mistakes as God's

chosen people, the Israelites are overthrown by the Babylonians, and many of their people are exiled to Babylon. King Nebuchadnezzar has a giant gold statue made of himself and commands the people to bow down to it.

Three faithful, God-fearing Israelites—Shadrach, Meshach, and Abednego—refuse to follow this command. To these men, there is only One who deserves worship, and it sure isn't the king of Babylon. Their conviction causes them to resist the king's decree, and as a result, they face the consequence: incineration in a fiery furnace.

Keep in mind, these heroes don't know that they will be saved from death in this circumstance when they say to Nebuchadnezzar: "If our God whom we serve is able to deliver us from the furnace of blazing fire and out of your hand, O king, let him deliver us. But if not, be it known to you, O king, that we will not serve your gods and we will not worship the golden statue that you have set up."[2] They would rather die than be seen worshipping something other than God!

I don't know if I would have made the same choice if I'd been faced with a fiery furnace of death. I would have been tempted to pretend to worship Nebuchadnezzar, but in secret remain faithful to God. But Shadrach, Meshach, and Abednego demonstrate that actions speak louder than words. Like Chill, they refuse to bow down to a dictator attempting to control them. While Chell is inspired by the hope of freedom, the three Israelites refuse to obey Nebuchadnezzar because of their conviction that only God is to be worshipped. They have an alternative allegiance that is more important to them than life among the Babylonians.

Rather than burn up when they're thrown in the

flames, Shadrach, Meshach, and Abednego are completely unharmed, and an angelic figure appears in the furnace with them. Nebuchadnezzar is astonished, and, unlike GLaDOS, humbles himself, acknowledging their high regard for their God: "They disobeyed the king's command and yielded up their bodies rather than serve and worship any god except their own God."[3]

While the majority of Christians in the Western world do not face deathly challenges like this, I wonder how often we compromise our values, even a little bit at a time, because they aren't popular values to have. It has certainly been easy for me to deny or omit my faith in Christ when I'm in certain groups, especially when my faith would make me an outsider. There have been times where I've stood by and pretended—whether overtly or otherwise—that my faith was non-existent. I've chosen to "worship" the Nebuchadnezzars of the world rather than stand up for God and face the social consequences.

I see at least two ways the protagonists of Daniel effectively stand up to social pressure.

First, they are in community together. The book doesn't mention the dialogue between them, but I can imagine a situation where one of the three Israelites feels a little less faithful, while the other two are saying, "Don't give up on the true God! God is the one who's got your back!"

Second, they refuse to disobey God's commandment that "you shall have no other gods before me."[4] They are given, by God, "knowledge and skill in every aspect of literature and wisdom."[5] They learn the skills and tools of the empire, but they do not comply with the ultimate allegiance the empire asks of them. Instead, they choose to practice patient defiance, similar to Chell.

Chell is an example of a "silent protagonist," meaning she doesn't speak at all for the duration of the video game. While the main point of this trait is to make you, as a player, feel like you are stepping into her shoes, it also serves as patient defiance of the incessant taunts and jabs that GLaDOS makes. When faced with a difficult situation with no escape, she *makes* her own way out through the power of portals—she uses the "wisdom" she has learned through the challenges. This encourages me that, when I face situations day-to-day with seemingly no good way to escape, I should use the tools and wisdom God has given me to bring me to safety. Of course, it's not always simple. Sometimes, we don't have the tools. Sometimes, we fail. But, in faith, we persevere.

These characters stand firm in their convictions, refusing to bend to an imperial and idolatrous authority that tells them to do something against their will (and their faith).

My prayer is that we all would have even a shred of Shadrach, Meshach, Abednego, and Chell's conviction in our daily interactions, and that we would stand firm in our beliefs, despite the fires of the world around us. We don't have a Portal Gun to help us escape from such situations, but we do have the promises of a God who loves us (even more than GLaDOS and Nebuchadnezzar love themselves).

Our God is worth stepping into the flames for.

Key Scripture

> "Blessed is anyone who endures temptation. Such a one has stood the test and will receive the crown of life that the Lord has promised to those who love him." —James 1:12

Reflection Questions

> 1. What kind of "incinerators" have you found yourself facing lately, in which you've felt pressures demanding you deny or ignore God? How have you responded in those situations?
>
> 2. What actions are you taking to ensure that you have a community of Christ-followers to lean on in difficult times?
>
> 3. Have you felt surprised when encountering an obstacle in your faith, or realized you might have to sacrifice something for your beliefs? Why or why not?

---

1. *Portal*. Microsoft Windows, Valve, 2007.
2. Daniel 3:17–18.
3. Daniel 3:28.
4. Exodus 20:3.
5. Daniel 1:17.

11

THOR IS STILL WORTHY AND SO ARE YOU

BY JASON DUECK

"I'm still worthy."
—Thor, *Avengers: Endgame*[1]

Read: Romans 8

Reflect: If anyone knows pain and suffering, it's Thor. In his quest to become a leader worthy of his legacy, his mother is killed in front of him; his prized weapon, Mjolnir, is smooshed like wet cardboard; he is forced to sacrifice his entire realm to stop the genocide of his people; and, in the opening scene of *Infinity War*, he's brutally beaten by Thanos and left floating, near death, in space.

Even after he succeeds in his quest to find a new weapon powerful enough to kill Thanos once and for all, he fails to stop the snap that eradicates half of all life in the galaxy. It's no wonder that when we meet Thor in *Endgame*, he is deep in the throes of denial and depression. He failed, and billions, perhaps trillions, across the galaxy paid the price for it.

It's only when he returns to his home, Asgard, in a previous timeline that a spark is once again kindled in him. His mother—still alive in this timeline—assures him that failing doesn't make him a failure: "Everyone fails at who they're 'supposed' to be, Thor. The measure of a person, a hero, is how well they succeed at being who they are."

Just before he returns to his prime timeline, Thor reaches out his hand and waits. Suddenly, Mjolnir—his mighty hammer and the truest test of a hero's worth—flies to his hand once again. In excited disbelief, he whispers, "I'm still worthy."

While I haven't suffered in the ways Thor has, I've certainly felt unworthy. I can't count the number of times I've failed and felt ashamed. When I'm rude to or short with my wife, I feel unworthy to be her husband. When I miss a deadline or make a mistake, I feel unworthy to have my job. When I sin, I feel unworthy to be loved by God.

And, like Thor, I often fall into the false and dangerous line of thinking that I have to accomplish some great act of redemption to earn again the worth I believe I've previously earned. Even after his mighty lightning-slinging hammer returns to him, Thor still believes he needs to be the one to wield the Infinity Gauntlet and undo Thanos's plan, though the Hulk is clearly more properly equipped for the job.

He pleads to the other Avengers, "Just let me do it. Just let me do something good. Something right." He killed Thanos, sure, but it didn't undo his own mistakes. He reasons that risking everything to wield the cosmic power of the Gauntlet and return the lost billions to life—this single act of heroism—might overwrite his many failures. Even after Mjolnir has shown him his worth, he is stuck in the belief that he must continue to earn it.

In Psalm 139, the psalmist writes that God knows my innermost parts before I am born. God knows all the good and bad I will be, but still loves me. In Romans 5:8, Paul writes that Jesus' death on the cross is proof of God's love. And in Romans 8, Paul states, in no uncertain terms, that there is nothing that can separate me from the love of Christ.

God tells me my worth is not tied to anything I have done or can ever do. It is, in fact, quite the opposite. I have been imbued with worth as the creation of the Creator. My value can no more be separate from me than the saltiness of salt. I am worthy exclusively because God has made me worthy. No action I could ever take will make me more or less valuable in the eyes of our loving Creator.

This is absolutely revolutionary compared to the understanding of worth Thor, and many of us, live in.

When we make mistakes—and we make plenty—God tells us we're no less worthy of love. Period. Full stop. No buts.

In Thor's story, his worthiness is derived from his deeds. He earns Mjolnir's power by acting heroically. And to keep his worth, he must keep acting heroically. Even though Mjolnir finds Thor worthy, Thor doesn't believe he is. But how much more good and loving than Mjolnir is God?

It's easy to accept a half measure of this truth in Christian life. We tell ourselves that no mistake can make God love us less, and when we lose our temper or slip into unhealthy habits, we believe God is waiting for us with open arms.

But when it's something more extreme, do we still believe we've been called worthy? Do we draw a line in the sand for certain sins, judging ourselves, or others, harshly because we've crossed a line? The fact is, the worst thing you've done has no effect on your worth. The worst thing you could ever do has no effect on your worth.

There is no distance, no depth, no earthly ruler, no angel, no demon, no life, no death, nothing present and nothing to come that can ever, for a second, separate you from the worth you have to God. You can't out-bad God's goodness. Your greatest mistake will not make a dent in the Creator's forgiveness.

You are worthy to wield all the power and love God has for you. Unlike Thor, you can't possibly earn it. But, like Thor, all you need to do is reach out to God and know that you are worthy.

Key Scripture

"Are not two sparrows sold for a penny? Yet not one of them will fall to the ground apart from your Father. And even the hairs of your head are all counted. So do not be afraid; you are of more value than many sparrows." —Matthew 10:29–31

Study Questions

1. What voices in your life do you let determine your worth?

2. When was the last time you did something to try to "earn" God's acceptance?

3. Consider how your life would look differently if you lived completely in the belief that you've been made worthy by God. What's one step you can take today to move towards that?

---

1. *Avengers: Endgame*. Directed by Anthony and Joe Russo. Walt Disney Studios, 2019.

12

LIFE, DEATH, AND SCYTHE

BY DUSTIN SCHELLENBERG

"2042. It's the year that every schoolchild knows. It was the year when computational power became infinite—or so close to infinite that it could no longer be measured. It was the year we knew... everything.... But like so many things, once we had possession of infinite knowledge, it suddenly seemed less important. Less urgent. Yes, we know everything, but I often wonder if anyone bothers to look at all that knowledge."

—*Scythe* by Neal Shusterman[1]

Read: James 3:13–18

Reflect: In Neal Shusterman's novel *Scythe,* the world exists as a "utopia," thanks to an AI called the Thunderhead. The Thunderhead was created to be gracious, kind, and benevolent to a fault. Through its vast wisdom, there are no longer diseases, plagues, or pandemics. Old age has become a thing of the past, as anyone can reset their age (called "turning the corner") to any age after mid-20s. The logistics of food production are completely handled by the Thunderhead, so hunger is no longer a problem. Poverty is alleviated with a standard living wage, although people can pursue more prestigious jobs for greater wealth if they wish.

Even accidental death is rendered obsolete, as the memories and experiences of people are constantly uploaded into the Thunderhead. Short of full destruction down to the cellular level or lower (such as death by fire or acid), anyone can be reconstructed. But even if the body is gone forever, people can engage with their memories, which live on in artificial constructs. Access to all knowledge has allowed people to overcome almost everything that sets humanity back.

Yet the world is not good. Boredom leads people to do greater and greater acts of self-destruction until they eventually settle for a bland existence. There are professional partiers who are available to fulfill one's entertainment needs. Many people go through a period of extreme living where they jump off buildings, over-consume, or participate in other destructive actions. Most people indulge in whatever they feel like.

All the knowledge in the world, via access to infinite computing, does not remove selfishness. It ends up making people care less about what happens around them. Apart from intimate friends and family, other lives mean nothing to most people. The knowledge of the infinite is largely wasted on entertainment, and few, if any, better themselves or seek to better the world.

For all its greatness, the wisdom of the Thunderhead cannot escape what the Bible calls "earthly, unspiritual, devilish" wisdom.[2] Even though the Thunderhead seeks to improve humanity, people still focus on their own selfish desires. The Thunderhead must constantly work to mitigate humanity's selfishness. Overindulgence, cruel ambition, and carelessness are constant problems that must be addressed. Although the Thunderhead largely manages these things, there is one problem the Thunderhead can't solve: over-population.

In response to a "deathless" world, the first generation to crack the code to eternal life, alongside the Thunderhead, form an agency called the Scythdom, which gleans (kills) a certain percentage of the population every year. For all the wisdom of humankind, death is still required for their survival. The Scythdom leads many people to fear death, as this journal entry from the novel relates:

"The woman I gleaned today asked me the oddest question.

'Where do I go now?' she asked.

'Well,' I explained calmly, 'your memories and life recording are already stored in the Thunderhead so it won't be lost. Your body is returned to the earth in a manner determined by your next of kin.'

'Yes, I know all that,' she said. 'But what about me?'

The question perplexed me. 'As I said, your memory construct will exist in the Thunderhead. Loved ones will be able to talk to it, and your construct will respond.'

'Yes,' she said, getting a bit agitated, 'but what about *me?*'

I gleaned her then. Only after she was gone did I say, 'I don't know.'"

The fear of death is deeply tied to the self-indulgent world humanity has created, not because death might hurt, but because what happens next is out of their control. The drive to feel, experience, and have is central to the world of *Scythe* (and our own world as well) and entirely under the control of the individual. Death is a loss of control. No matter what comes next, in a world that has maximized autonomy and taken away almost all the repercussions for being selfish, that is terrifying. Although the world is largely known, and even though most people eventually fall into apathy, at least they know what to expect.

The combined knowledge of humanity and the Thunderhead's computing power is so different from what James calls "wisdom from above."[3] In God's eyes, being wise means giving up control and accepting God's direction. It means valuing peace, love, and sacrifice over self-indulgence. It means being gracious and merciful. It means pursuing justice and choosing gentleness. It means putting no one above another, seeking to make decisions that benefit everybody. It means seeking reconciliation and looking for good in bad situations.

All the knowledge in the world can't produce that type of wisdom.

In a strange way, the author of Ecclesiastes comes to this same realization: a good life is one in which you take pleasure in the little things and love others. Do things to the best of your ability and, when the time comes, rest.

The advice in Ecclesiastes seems to be the opposite of the narratives we are used to—stories that tell us to change the world, be the big player, be the hero. But Christ doesn't call us to be the centre of attention. We don't need to be known by the world, only by God. Do good things. Let go of selfish ambition and take joy in the day-to-day life with others. Find contentment in God and loving others, and there will be little to fear in death, because the need to know everything and find total fulfillment isn't essential. God invites us to find true joy in creating a better world and then resting in a future that God promises, and over which we have no control.

James and the author of Ecclesiastes both recognize that the best thing we do is pass on seeds of goodness that grow even after we're gone. Where the Thunderhead's type of wisdom elevates the individual above all else and seeks to be the pinnacle of all things, Godly wisdom plants goodness that will create a harvest much later. It creates lasting legacies of hope and peace. God's wisdom redefines success as making the world a better place for everyone instead of raising up a single individual. And it does not require our own knowledge or allowances for selfishness. *Scythe* never solves this problem.

In *Scythe*, the fear of death and selfish ambition are never overcome. Under humanity's power, even with an infinite AI, the best they can accomplish is figuring out a different way to let everyone do what they want. The fear of death still stands, even if its necessity is diminished. Thankfully, the wisdom of God gives us another vantage point from where we can be content in letting go of selfish ambition and the need to be at the center of everything.

We are free to accept what comes, be kind and good to others, and live at peace with our own finiteness.

Key Scripture

> "Go, eat your bread with enjoyment, and drink
> your wine with a merry heart; for God has long
> ago approved what you do. Let your garments
> always be white; do not let oil be lacking on your
> head. Enjoy life with the wife whom you love, all
> the days of your vain life that are given you under
> the sun, because that is your portion in life and in
> your toil at which you toil under the sun. What-
> ever your hand finds to do, do with your might; for
> there is no work or thought or knowledge or
> wisdom in Sheol, to which you are going."
> —Ecclesiastes 9:7–10

Study Questions

1. Are you afraid of dying? Why or why not?

2. We are used to stories that tell us to do big
things. How can you apply James's narrative to
your life instead?

3. What is a simple, good thing you can do this
week to live in the wisdom from above?

---

1. Shusterman, Neal. *Scythe*. Simon & Schuster, 2016.
2. James 3:15.
3. James 3:15.

13

EVERY RED SHIRT HAS A NAME

BY KYLE RUDGE

"I was briefed on the details surrounding your last [captain]. I know he betrayed this crew. If I were you, I would have doubts about me too."
—Christopher Pike, *Star Trek: Discovery*[1]

Read: Matthew 18:1–5; 10–14

Reflect: Star Trek is known for its iconic captains, such as Kirk, Picard, Sisko, Janeway, and Archer. Each of their respective series revolves around their exploits. They are the heroic figureheads of their ships (or stations), so when the captain in *Star Trek: Discovery*'s first season turns out to be a villain, it is profoundly revolutionary to the traditions of the franchise.

In Season Two, the crew of the *Discovery* is recovering from the trauma of being betrayed by someone they trusted, though the experience also formed strong bonds between them. First Officer Ceru has stepped up and taken on the role of acting captain. He has proven himself to the crew and they have complete trust and confidence in him.

Enter, Captain Christopher Pike.

Pike takes command of the *Discovery* under Star Fleet's orders, citing "Regulation 19, Section C" after he is beamed aboard. Immediately, Ceru questions Pike's authority:

> **Ceru:** "Forgive me, Captain. Your directive is only instituted under three contingencies: when an imminent threat is detected, when the lives of Federation citizens are in danger, or when no other officers of equal or higher rank are present to mitigate this threat. May I ask under which contingency you are here?"
> **Pike:** "All of them."

Once on the bridge, Pike does something shocking; the scene is one of the best analogies of the gospel I have ever seen.

While transferring command of the *Discovery* to Pike on the bridge and having his DNA verified, Pike's private personnel profile accidentally comes onto the main screen for all to see. Pike is not dismayed by it; instead, he instructs the crew to have a seat and read everything in the file. He basks in this vulnerability, even though he knows that any slight discrepancy, any yellow flag, any question raised by the crew about his file could completely destroy the already tense relationship he has with them.

Pike glosses over the commendations in his file and instead points out his humanity—the diagnosis of child-hood asthma and his failing grade in Astrophysics at the

Academy. He turns to look at everyone and names the elephant in the room.

> "I was briefed on the details surrounding your last [captain]. I know he betrayed this crew. If I were you, I would have doubts about me too."

By beginning his command with honesty and respect, he takes a step toward gaining their trust. He then debriefs them on their mission with the understanding that trust takes time and action, not just words.

After their ship warps to the mission location, Pike does something else strange. He says, "Bridge crew, give me a roll call."

At these words, everyone on the bridge looks at each other, confused. Fans of the Star Trek franchise might be baffled as well. It is a well-known fact that many crew members on Star Trek shows are unnamed (the red shirts that are expendable, for example). And yet, Pike wants to know the names of everyone under his command.

> "Lord knows what is waiting for us down there. I want to know who I am facing it with. Sound off. And skip your ranks; they don't matter," he says.

Ranks don't matter to Pike, but names do. People do. Every single person in the room gives their name (and we are learning some of their names for the first time, even though they were present throughout the first season). As we come to learn in the remainder of the season, every person here also has a story worth exploring.

Star Trek: Discovery isn't your parents' Star Trek. It's something entirely new.

After the roll call, Pike issues orders using the crew's first names instead of their ranks. For a moment, there is calm and a foundation of respect being built. Then they drop out of warp and discover a crashed Starfleet ship on an asteroid—a ship thought destroyed years ago.

> **Pike:** "Any life signs?"
> **Burnham:** "Still impossible to scan, sir."

Pike immediately goes into crisis-solving mode, commanding the crew to prep a landing party and brainstorming ideas on how to get there. The crew protest his plans because of the dangerous gravity fields and the likelihood that no one is alive down there anyway.

Pike objects, "If anyone is down there, I am not leaving them there to die!"

Ceru voices what is written on everyone else's faces:

> "It is my duty to articulate that the odds of survival in a crashed ship on one of the most hostile environments in space are unlikely. And risking more crew to confirm that fact, well, it requires consideration."

Without hesitation, Pike shuts Ceru down. Failure is not an option. Consideration is not even an option. And it is in that moment that I fell in love with Pike as captain.

Jesus tells the Parable of the Lost Sheep in Matthew 18 and Luke 15. In this story, a shepherd chases after the one sheep that has gone astray in a large flock. He values that sheep just as much as the others, because it is not just a number to him.

Similarly, on Pike's ship are many highly qualified, highly valuable sheep with names. In this situation, there was only the *possibility* of a lost sheep. And even then, there was no objection too strong, no obstacle too great, no consideration worth exploring that would keep this shepherd from going after it. Why? Because that sheep also has a name. That sheep also has a story.

In Luke 15, Jesus is sitting with a group of people that the religious people considered deplorable:

> "Now all the tax collectors and sinners were coming near to listen to him. And the Pharisees and the scribes were grumbling and saying, 'This fellow welcomes sinners and eats with them.'"[2]

Jesus speaks to them and cites the parable. He implies that the religious leaders and the teachers of the law are not excluded from being a part of the flock. Despite their misunderstanding and dismissing of the deplorable, they are still children of God. Jesus challenges their assumption that a redshirt is nameless and invaluable. To God, everyone has a name and a story worth celebrating.

To Christopher Pike, the mere possibility that one person was alive onboard a ship heading towards destruction meant he had to go after them.

It's easy to ignore the humanity of someone you don't know. Pike could have done that, citing his crew's safety as more important. He reminds me of all the times I've looked away from a homeless person, trying not to acknowledge their humanity or that they have a story of their own. He reminds me that the few times I have asked a stranger their name, their story suddenly mattered to me. Seeing others as human, just as valuable as we are, can start with something as simple as that. What is your name? Skip your rank; it doesn't matter.

Key Scripture

> "Do not fear, for I have redeemed you; I have called you by name, you are mine." —Isaiah 43:1

Reflection Questions:

1. Have you ever felt like your name or story did not matter to someone? What feelings did that cause?

2. Has a stranger ever called you by name? If so, what did that feel like? If not, what do you imagine it would feel like?

3. Does knowing how Christ values everyone change your perspective in how you encounter strangers? If you knew their name and their story, would your perspective change? Why or why not?

---

1. *Star Trek: Discovery.* "Brother," season 2, episode 1. Directed by Alex Kurtzman. CBS Television, 2019.
2. Luke 15:1–2.

14

HOPE LIVES: SAMURAI JACK AND FINDING FREEDOM IN FORGIVENESS

BY ALLISON ALEXANDER

"Hope lives. It is everywhere. I've seen it—everyone you have touched, people you have helped. You saved them."

—Ashi, *Samurai Jack*[1]

Read: 1 Peter 1

Reflect:[2] If anyone is familiar with regretting the past, it's the samurai who's lost his purpose. Returning after thirteen years since the show originally concluded on Cartoon Network, *Samurai Jack*'s fifth season continues the story of a man who was thrown into a future ruled by the evil Aku. Jack's mission is to return to the past to stop the villain from overtaking the world, something he's been unable to accomplish so far.

In the new season, Jack's spirit is broken. It's been fifty years since the events of the previous season, though he hasn't aged. "Time has lost its effect on me," he says in the series intro. "Yet, the suffering continues."

Aku has destroyed all the remaining time portals, stranding Jack in the apocalyptic future. Jack feels guilty and ashamed because it was his destiny to bring hope to the world. In episode six, he is ready to give up. A samurai ghost called "The Omen" calls out his guilt and demands punishment for his failure. Jack is prepared to die.

Jack reflects the hopelessness that past sin and failure can inflict in the present. It's easy to dwell on the mistakes we've made and continue to punish ourselves for them. Especially in Christian culture, there are certain sins that are mistakenly treated as unforgivable—inflicting pain in others and betrayal are often included among these. It's when we let the people we love down that others (and often ourselves) feel we deserve to suffer indefinitely for our crimes. While our actions do have consequences, the point of forgiveness is that we might not deserve it, but we're given it anyway.

In Jack's case, he feels like he has failed people, but the opposite is true. Ashi, who used to be Aku's minion but is now Jack's friend, spends most of the episode meeting many of the people Jack impacted during previous episodes. Throwbacks to the original series abound as she encounters the Woolies, whom Jack freed from slavery in Season One; the three blind archers, whose curse he broke and who are now part of a resistance against Aku; the children, now adults, Jack liberated from a mind-controlling DJ in Season Three; and the wannabe samurai from Season Four that he saved from self-destruction.

"Hope lives. It is everywhere. I've seen it—everyone you have touched, people you have helped. You saved them," Ashi says to Jack as he sits defeated on the ground, ready to meet his death.

All the beings he impacted recognize the hope he has brought them and are incredibly thankful for it. They move Ashi to a closer understanding of what truth and self-sacrifice looks like. Now it is someone else's turn to bring hope to Jack.

Sometimes, we don't recognize the impact we have on other people. If we spend time making relationships a priority, being kind to others and treating them as Christ would, that effort may reap joy later on. Even if we don't see the impact of our actions in the same way that Jack does, that doesn't mean we give up.

In the Bible, the apostle Peter writes to a group of Christians, likely both Jews and Gentiles, who are modeling their lives after Christ and standing out as aliens or "exiles" because of it.[3] He speaks about persecution, likely anticipating the hardships Christians would face in the final years of Nero's reign. Peter encourages the believers to continue living well, even though they are suffering for their actions.

"Live in reverent fear during the time of your exile," Peter advises,[4] suggesting that Christians should hope and trust in God, understanding the Creator is holy and they should try to model that to the best of their abilities. Love one another, Peter tells them. Love others deeply and from the heart.

This type of love is exactly what Jack has modeled throughout the series, but he has lost his hope during his exile. Thankfully, Ashi is there to remind him of the power of forgiveness and of relinquishing past sins.

Ashi's character arc is even more redemption-filled than Jack's. Her entire life up to this point was spent training as an assassin for Aku. The high priestess who trained her describes her as "the strongest, but the most unfocused. Always distracted, questioning everything," as if questioning her beliefs is a bad thing.

On the contrary, Ashi's willingness to explore truth is what makes her strong. Though she stubbornly clings to her servitude towards Aku during the first few episodes of Season Five, Jack patiently provides her with proof of the villain's terror-filled reign. Ashi confronts her beliefs and lets herself be changed by the truth; her shifting perspective is represented visually as she literally changes her appearance—washing off her black bodysuit and constructing a vibrant outfit made of leaves.

Her new attitude doesn't undo her past, but her acknowledgement that she was wrong and her determination to stand up for what's right in the future helps her accept it and move on.

During the middle of a fight, after Jack loses his sword, Ashi picks up the horn from the skeleton of an innocent creature that Jack had accidentally killed. She uses it to fight the high priestess and deflects an arrow that would have killed Jack. It's a symbolic moment as Jack is going through the process of forgiving himself for that mistake and for other past failures. He finds peace by confronting the past:

> "You. You are the one who has kept the past hidden," he tells an avatar of himself—a representation of his anger, fear, and doubt. "Your anger, your frustration... You have blinded us, but now I can see."[5]

It's easy to dwell in the past and let it define our future; thinking this way takes the responsibility of change off our shoulders. It's tempting because change is hard. It's simpler to fall into past habits and not make the effort to confront the truth of our transgressions. It's easy to stop trying, to ignore God's call to holy living. Forgiving ourselves is difficult, and accepting forgiveness from others can be just as challenging. Luckily, we have someone who offers to take the burden of our past sins for us: Jesus Christ.

It can take time, reflection, and experiencing more failures to get to the point where we're ready to ask for help and forgiveness, and that's okay. Christ is waiting.

The past is part of who we are, but it doesn't need to define our future. Like Jack and Ashi, we can confront our failures, our anger, our guilt and frustration, and move forward with the knowledge that we are forgiven. We continue to act, in faith and hope, like the people Peter wrote to in his letter, loving one another, loving deeply and from the heart.

Even in dark places hope can be found, though sometimes it needs to be pointed out to us by others, similar to how Peter encourages the recipients of his letter and Ashi encourages Jack. With the support of other believers and the knowledge that we are loved by an almighty Creator, we can move forward instead of constantly going back, back to the past. Samurai Jack.

Key Scripture

"I am [the One] who blots out your transgressions for my own sake, and I will not remember your sins." —Isaiah 43:25

Study Questions

> 1. Is there a failure in your past that you still think about? Have you forgiven yourself for it?
>
> 2. Can you think of a time when you felt like giving up, like Jack, but someone encouraged you to have hope?
>
> 3. How can you be like Ashi or Peter and encourage someone else this week?

---

1. *Samurai Jack*. "Episode XCVII," season 5, episode 6. Directed by Genndy Tartakovsky. Warner Bros., 2017.
2. A version of this devotional first appeared as an article on *Christ and Pop Culture*.
3. 1 Peter 1:1.
4. 1 Peter 1:17.
5. *Samurai Jack*. "Episode XCVIII," season 5, episode 7. Directed by Genndy Tartakovsky. Warner Bros., 2017.

15

VIOLET EVERGARDEN AND THE PURPOSE OF PAIN

BY SHANEEN THOMPSON

"Violet. Your name's Violet. I have a feeling you'll grow into it. You'll become much more than a weapon of war."

—Major Gilbert Bougainvillea, *Violet Evergarden*[1]

Read: Genesis 37, 41

Reflect: In the eighth episode of the anime TV show *Violet Evergarden*, a nameless child soldier is found on the front lines and "gifted" to Major Gilbert Bougainvillea by his older brother. Tenderhearted Gilbert is shocked by his brother's treatment of this child and horrified that he is expected to use her as a weapon.

"Gil, she's no child," his brother tells him. "She's just a weapon... A tool, for the purpose of war."

Since the girl has shown violent tendencies and terrifying skills, the army is eager to use her to their advantage; they believe "the only thing she's valuable for is killing."

Gilbert reluctantly follows his orders, but he sees

greater value in the child. He cares for her, teaches her to read and write, and helps her learn what it means to be human. He also names her, an act that humanizes her: "Violet. Your name's Violet. I have a feeling you'll grow into it. You'll become much more than a weapon of war." Naming her after a flower is significant because a flower's purpose is beauty, it suggests innocence, and it has nothing to do with war; violet petals are also shaped like hearts, which symbolize love, emotions, and healing.

Hoping to bring an end to the war, the army plans a pivotal mission to take over the enemy's headquarters. It is a difficult battle, but they are able to infiltrate the base with the aid of Violet's special skills. However, Gilbert is shot and mortally wounded.

As the story continues in episode 9, "Violet Evergarden," Violet tries to save Gilbert but is wounded herself and loses both her arms. When the defeated enemy bombs their own headquarters, Gilbert's final act is to push Violet to safety, telling her she needs to live and that he loves her.

Violet wakes up in an army hospital with mechanical prosthetics in place of her lost arms. She has much to come to terms with in her life now: the war is over and she is no longer needed in battle, the only place she knows she is skilled; she has lost her arms and is no longer able to do all the things she once could; and though she is unaware of Gilbert's death, she does know he is no longer there to instruct her. She has lost everything important to her, everything that defined her.

Violet is taken in by Claudia Hodgins, an army friend of the Major, and given a job as an Auto Memory Doll— someone who writes letters for people who are unable to or who desire assistance putting their thoughts and emotions into words. While she is unable to write with a quill, Violet is proficient with the tool of an Auto Memory Doll: the typewriter. Through her work and her search to understand Gilbert's final words, she becomes better at understanding and articulating human emotions. She writes some of the most beautiful letters in the country and is highly sought after for her skills as a Doll.

Despite the good that has come from her experiences, Violet's past haunts her. Upon learning that Gilbert has been declared Missing In Action and is presumed dead, she is tempted to give up. Working to come to terms with her suffering, she asks Hodgins if someone like her really deserves to keep living. Hodgins tells her that all the bad that she's done and all the bad that has happened to her cannot be erased. But neither can all the good that she is accomplishing now.

There is a character in the Bible who also experiences much suffering and knows what it's like to be abused and mistreated. Joseph is the beloved of twelve sons and his father favours him. He interprets his own dreams to mean that one day his parents and brothers will bow down to him. His brothers are jealous and plot to get rid of him. Luckily, the plan that started out as murder is downgraded to throwing him in a pit. Then, unluckily, that plan is upgraded to selling him into slavery when a caravan on its way to Egypt happens to pass by. Joseph's brothers tell their father that he was killed by wild animals, and they believe Joseph is out of their lives for good.

Joseph's life as a slave has some serious ups and downs, but he does some great things during this time and becomes important to Pharaoh himself. His story even has a happy ending, in which he is reunited with his family and forgives his brothers. His whole family moves to Egypt so that Joseph can provide for them.

Joseph suffers and goes through many hardships but recognizes that "Even though you intended to do harm to me, God intended it for good, in order to preserve a numerous people, as he is doing today."[2]

Life is hard. There are the typical daily nuisances, the inescapable tragedies of life, and the long seasons where the whole world seems to be against us. There are times when we are hurt by those around us, sometimes even by those closest to us. Predicaments can blindside us and it seems impossible to find any hope.

But even though we may not be able to see it, hope can be found in the worst of situations.

Violet experiences a lot of pain and loss, and while that pain can never be completely forgotten, she still has the opportunity to help others. I'm sure Joseph never completely forgets the hurt and the injustices he suffers, but those events put him in a position to do immense amounts of good. Both have a choice in how they react to what has happened to them.

In the midst of hardships, it's difficult to see how God is at work. Eager to find purpose in our suffering, we ask, "Why is this happening to me?" If we knew there was a reason and a greater purpose to our pain, maybe we could stand up under it better. We want something to make our suffering worth it. But finding purpose in pain isn't about making suffering "worth it."

The world is a broken place, and bad stuff happens. Sometimes, a difficult situation leads to amazing things: discovering a specific purpose for your life, finding an ability to uniquely connect with and support others, or growing as a person. But other times, we may never "see" any good come from it, or if we do, it may not seem like it's enough.

We don't always get a clear answer about why we must endure certain things in life. Sometimes life just sucks and the only thing we can do is trust that God cares and make the best decisions we can within our circumstances. God's purposes may not always be revealed as clearly as in Joseph's life, but God is at work in our suffering. Good can come out of even the greatest pain. I find hope in God's promise that suffering doesn't have the last word. Instead, the last word is love—the type of love Violet learns to project in her letters, the type of love that Joseph chooses to give to his brothers, and the type of love that God bestows upon us.

Key Scripture

> "We also boast in our sufferings, knowing that
> suffering produces endurance, and endurance
> produces character, and character produces hope,
> and hope does not disappoint us, because God's
> love has been poured into our hearts through the
> Holy Spirit that has been given to us."
> —Romans 5:3–5

Study Questions

1. Have you experienced hardships that you can look back on now and see how God was with you?

2. Are you experiencing hardships now that are difficult to understand? How can you hold onto God's truths during this time?

3. How does your suffering put you in a position to support those around you who are also struggling?

---

1. *Violet Evergarden.* Season 1, episode 8. Directed by Haruka Fujita et. al. Funimation, 2018.
2. Genesis 50:20.

16

METROID AND THE STATIONARY MOVEMENT OF GRACE

BY AARON THIESSEN

"As for me, one life ended... yet I survived, reborn as something different."
    —Samus Aran, *Metroid Fusion*[1]

Read: Ephesians 2:1–10

Reflect: I was a latecomer to the *Metroid* party. Though the first game came out in 1986, I didn't experience the series myself until 2002 with the release of *Metroid Prime*. Immediately, I was hooked. The sci-fi aesthetic, the solitary atmosphere, the emphasis on exploration and discovery—not to mention the relentless collecting of upgrades—all culminated in the video game franchise I never knew I wanted.

All *Metroid* titles follow a similar formula. The player steps into the role of Samus Aran, a famous, intergalactic bounty hunter. Samus faces a variety of antagonists—the titular Metroid parasites, the marauding Space Pirates, or her own doppelgänger—and it's always up to her to stop them.

While on her missions, Samus's greatest resource is her suit of power armour—an endlessly upgradeable, alien-crafted marvel of technology. This armour allows Samus to withstand harsh environments, jump to impossible heights, contract to the size of a soccer ball, and fire beams of cryogenic energy from her integrated arm cannon.

All this might suggest that *Metroid* is a series about combat, but that's actually not the case. These games are more about Samus's lonely exploration of hostile alien environments. The bulk of the player's adventure involves acquiring more and more ways to traverse the world and enter new areas. A sea of lava stands at the edge of the map? Find the suit upgrade to withstand the heat. A scan reveals the tunnel is blocked by a bendezium deposit? Find the power bomb upgrade and discover what secrets it holds. That last conflict with the Space Pirates didn't go so well? Look for some more missile upgrades and energy tanks to boost Samus's abilities. This continues over and over until, by the end of the game, virtually nothing can stop Samus' Herculean abilities.

Ironically, this power scaling creates a problem for the *Metroid* series' many sequels. If Samus ends one game as a demi-god, brushing aside even deadly obstacles with ease, the next game requires her to somehow lose all those powers so the *Metroid* formula can happen all over again. Hence, what I'll call the "*Metroid* cycle": the recurring reasons that Samus loses her upgrades and has to start over in each game (Oh no! They were damaged in an explosion. Oh no! They were stolen by shape-shifting aliens. Oh no!

Samus was infected by radiation and needs a new suit to stay alive.)

On and on the cycle goes. It makes one feel for Samus, stuck on this endless, Sisyphean treadmill. She strives so hard to secure victory, yet there is always some setback stripping her of power, always some hidden force reviving her enemies, always something blocking her from finding peace.

The structure of this *Metroid* cycle is a useful illustration for something that is almost impossible to discuss these days: *sin*.

Now there's a word with baggage! For some, talk of sin may seem quaint or archaic. For others, this word is inextricably tied to spiritual trauma and abuse. Either way, sin is often an off-putting subject. But whatever one's history with the term, at its most basic, sin literally means "to miss the mark"—and we all fail to reach the ideal from time to time. Our actions can cause harm to ourselves, to others, to creation, and even to our relationship with God. Despite our best efforts, we all experience moments when our endeavors seem to count for nothing and our fatal flaws resurrect themselves. It may not be the loss of power armour's capabilities, but we may lose confidence or struggle with the lie that we have to be perfect to earn God's love.

Perhaps sin will take form as something innocuous, like a bad grade in class from lazy time management. Or maybe it'll be more insidious, like a habit that has grown in secret and now seems to have a life of its own. Maybe it's something accidental, like an injury done to another out of ignorance, and now a cherished relationship is in jeopardy. Whatever form it takes, we all experience times when we lack diligence, react according to our worst impulses, or end up doing nothing when we should have done *something*.

Like Samus's perennial loss of upgrades, it's not a matter of *if*—it's a matter of *when* and *how*.

Missing the mark never feels pleasant. Like the instigating loss in a *Metroid* game, we feel stripped—and so we might take a page from Samus's book and try to solve the problem ourselves. While Samus collects new upgrades—missile tanks, morph ball advancements, suit augments, and broader visor wavelengths—we try mustering new willpower, or praying more diligently, or testing out the latest self-help techniques.

And perhaps that striving works, for a while. But then, out of the blue, disaster will inevitably strike again: an outburst, a failure, an oversight, a relapse. The cycle starts all over again. Sin always has a sequel.

Yet this is precisely what grace is for, right? Isn't this exactly the message of Christianity? That Jesus died on the cross for our sin? Many of us have heard that line before, and it certainly seems to be the message of Ephesians 2:5—"Even when we were dead in our tresspasses, [God] made us alive together with Christ—by grace you have been saved."

Do we catch how radical these words actually are? From our perspective within the cycle, it's easy to think of God's grace as an infinite offering of second chances, as though God looks at sin and says, "I know you've made a mistake, but it will be okay; you can try again tomorrow." However, if this is all grace is, then the cycle stays intact—our actual realities don't yet meet the ideal; we're forgiven, but ultimate value is still placed on improving, on striving, on collecting the next proverbial energy tank and over-coming that final obstacle *ourselves*.

But what if grace is something more than this? What if the grace of Christ isn't about giving us permission to try to strive again tomorrow, and more about shattering the cycle by letting us be stationary?

What if grace means you *don't* need to muster the willpower to get somewhere; you *don't* need to find the right strength or power to overcome some obstacle; you *don't actually need to do anything at all* to be loved in the Divine eyes? We experience true grace when we simply accept the fact that we are accepted—and in that experi-ence, we may not be better than before, and we may not believe more than before, but everything is transformed.

Grace is not merely permission to try again tomorrow. Grace—real grace—is the moment we realize that the love of Christ completely covers even this moment, this break-down, this weakness, this *sin,* before we move at all. And ironically, it is exactly in this cycle-shattering experience of grace that true change can take place.

It would be akin to Samus starting a new adventure, losing her upgrades yet another time, and being shown in that moment that she doesn't need a souped up suit of power armour to change the world. She herself, in her vulnerability, is all that is required.

It would make for a terrible *Metroid* game. But it does make for good transformation.

Key Scripture

"Three times I appealed to the Lord about this

[torment], that it would leave me, but he said to me, 'My grace is sufficient for you, for power is made perfect in weakness.' So, I will boast all the more gladly of my weaknesses, so that the power of Christ may dwell in me." —2 Corinthians 12:8–9

Study Questions

1. To paraphrase Oscar Wilde, the only thing worse than not getting what you want is getting it. Is this true? How might this sentiment relate to our desire to strive, versus learning to be stationary?

2. As you were reading, what was your reaction to the word *sin*? What did it stir within you? Do you think your reaction might highlight a space that God desires to heal? Simply accept? Draw attention to? Repent of? Regardless of the answer, remember that grace is *already there*.

3. Although grace comes from God, it is also something we can embody for others. Is there a situation in your life where you can incarnate grace for someone else?

---

1. *Metroid Fusion*. Game Boy Advance, Nintendo, 2002.

17

THE GOOD PLACE AND IMPERFECT PEOPLE IN RELATIONSHIP

BY PHILIPPA ISOM

"We're asking the wrong question... it doesn't matter if people are good or bad, but what matters is if they are trying to be better than they were yesterday. Want to know where hope comes from—that's your answer."
—Michael, *The Good Place*[1]

Read: 1 Thessalonians 5

Reflect: When I first started watching *The Good Place*, I assumed it would be similar to other sitcoms—simple, brain candy entertainment. I was wrong. Although it certainly is good entertainment, *The Good Place* is filled with thought-provoking characters and quotes that invite watchers to participate in a larger conversation about life. One question in particular comes up again and again—is real change possible?

In Season One, Michael—a demon and the Good Place architect—attempts to build a unique torture chamber for humans. He wants to prove that demons can do better than the traditional techniques that they have been using for eternity (such as butthole spiders, penis flatteners, and Bad Janet's farts). He suggests that the torture humans can inflict on each other is far worse. However, rather than torture each other, his human test subjects—Eleanor, Chidi, Tahani, and Jason—work together to become better versions of themselves. Throughout the following seasons, they continue to persevere, even through the memory wipes and various experiments they are subjected to.

I experienced an "aha" moment when watching Season Three; Michael realizes that humans cannot win entry to the Good Place on individual point accumulation, no matter how hard they try, because the world is so complex:

> "In 1534, Douglas Winegar of England gave his grandmother roses for her birthday; he picked them himself, walked them over to her. She was happy. Boom—145 points. ... In 2009, Doug Euwing of Scagsville, Maryland, also gave his grandmother a dozen roses, but he lost four points. Why? Because he ordered roses using a cell phone that was made in a sweatshop; the flowers were grown with toxic pesticides and were picked by exploited migrant workers, delivered from thousands of miles away, which created a massive carbon footprint, and his money went to a billionaire racist CEO who sends his female employees pictures of his genitals! ... Don't you understand, the Bad Place isn't tampering with points. They don't have to, because every day the world gets a

little more complicated, and being a good person gets a little harder."[2]

The show not only explores the complexity of the world, but the complexity of human relationships. In Season Four, the characters realize that changing into better versions of themselves is not about the accumulation of personal points, but about their relationships and how they can support each other to change.

Take Eleanor and Chidi, for example. Eleanor begins as a selfish person with questionable morals. Her relationship with Chidi, a professor of ethics and moral philosophy, leads her to become a better version of herself. In every iteration of their relationship, Eleanor learns to consider others and become part of a community. Chidi also becomes a better version of himself because of their relationship. Eleanor helps him to see the lighter side of life and "chillax, man" rather than being consumed by indecision.

The other characters also uncover and come to value their own uniqueness. They focus on loving and supporting each other instead of helping themselves. It is through acceptance of their weaknesses—their own and each other's—that they all grow in strength. What starts out as a group of individuals trying to get enough points to be deemed "good enough" for the Good Place ends with a community willing to put eternity on the line for each other.

If there is one thing that I have learned as I have aged, it's that subscribing to the Western world's individualistic, meritocratic society does not bring me connection or joy. In the constant drive to be *the* best, I lose sight of becoming *my* best. I often forget that my best is tied up in the best of others.

From the very beginning of creation, God determined that it was not good for humans to be alone. Like the nature of God—a triune being in complete unity—humans are designed to be in relationship, both with God and with each other. After God created, God invited humanity to be co-creators on the earth in partnership with others.

Over and over through the biblical narrative, we humans have not played our part, and God has created an escape plan to bring us back into relationship. The opportunities for a "do-over" are reflected in the rebooting of the characters in *The Good Place*. In fact, Janet, the AI who is "not a robot and not a girl," becomes more sentient and closer to being a human every time she is rebooted. Might it be that every time we mess up and then come to God in repentance, we actually become closer to the original design for partnership? The same might be said of our relationships with others when we choose to "reboot" relationships and partner with each other to become better versions of ourselves.

Paul's letters to the church often address community and being together. 1 Thessalonians 5 is written in the context of "the day of the Lord,"[3] which many understand as the coming of Christ.[4] Both this passage and *The Good Place* reflect on human behaviour from the perspective of the end of life in the here and now as we know it.

In 1 Thessalonians 5:14, Paul specifically tells the Thessalonian church to "encourage one another and build each other up." Paul does not call the people to first pull each other down and rebuild from scratch, but to help each other. After the initial greetings and background about when Paul was in Thessalonica in person, the gist of the letter to the church is encouragement. Paul tells then that they are doing really well, makes some suggestions of what they could do better, and directs them to do these things together—to support each other so they can make the transition from previous un-Godly ways to the teachings of Jesus. It is with the support of each other that they will see where changes in their lives need to be made and then make those changes endure.

Change is not easy, especially sustained change. Our brains are wired to follow the path of least resistance, the patterns of behaviour that we've established over years of practice. In order to make a change, we have to practice the new action over and over again until the previous neural pathway is overgrown and our thoughts and behaviours are transformed. This is where the importance of support comes in.

I used to think being a "good" Christian was all about being perfect—following every word of the law, serving in every ministry, and pointing out where others were going wrong. I became legalistic, holding myself apart from "those other sinners." As I have matured, I have learned that Christians have been set free from the law and are guided by love:

"Owe no one anything, except to love one another; for the one who loves another has fulfilled the law," writes Paul in Romans 13:8.

It is through love and relationship with others that we are changed. It is through love that we are connected to community and, therefore, to each other. It is through love that we reject the ideas of the world about position and power and, instead, live transformed lives in which we support others.

Mana is a word in the Māori language that speaks of the dignity of a person. I have been transforming all of my interactions with people by asking the question, "is this mana enhancing?" The question reflects Paul's encouragement to "build each other up." I ask myself, does this way of being with someone, regardless of their actions or perceived status, enhance their mana? This change in thinking has been transformational for me, who was once rather a "hothead," much like Eleanor Shellstrop. It has not been easy and it has taken much repetition. But I am finally getting to a place where this is becoming my new normal.

Transformation takes time, a concept that is played with in a rather amusing way in Season Four of *The Good Place*. As Michael tries to explain how time works in the afterlife, it is made clear that time is not a linear progression. Similarly, in order to change, one must go up and down and back and forth. Change, like the Jeremy Bearimy timeline, is messy and complex and not straightforward. Plus, since time works as a loop in the afterlife, the concept of grace comes into play. You can always go back and take another run at something you got wrong. It's not always about the results of your actions; it's about your heart and trying to get a little bit better every day.

Getting into the Good Place is not about being perfect, just as being a Christian is not about being perfect. Rather, our relationship with God is about noticing what, in our lives, needs to be transformed and starting to work on that. Like in the Good Place, we do not have to do this alone. In fact, trying to be transformative as an individual is next to impossible in the highly complex and interwoven world we live in. We are called to be a unique part of the body to function where we are. That means learning to support the transformation of others as they also support us.

In the closing episode of *The Good Place*, Chidi gives some great advice for those on the journey of transformation: "Turns out life isn't a puzzle that can just be solved one time and it's done. You wake up everyday and you solve it again."[5]

Key Scripture

> "May the God of hope fill you with all joy and peace as you trust in him, so that you may overflow with hope by the power of the Holy Spirit."
> —Romans 15:13

Reflection Questions

1. How does your attitude toward life change if your goal is to be a little bit better each day instead of to reach perfection?

2. Are there areas in your life in need of change? Can you imagine this change and what support you might need in order to make it a sustained change?

3. How does this devotional relate to the one we read yesterday on grace and *Metroid*? Why should

we struggle to do good, improve, be in relationship
with others, and live transformed lives if grace
covers all our failures?

---

1. *The Good Place.* "A Chip Driver Mystery," season 4, episode 6.
   Directed by Steve Day. NBCUniversal, 2019.
2. *The Good Place.* "The Book of Dougs," season 3, episode 10.
   Directed by Ken Whittingham. NBCUniversal, 2019.
3. 1 Thessalonians 5:2.
4. 1 Thessalonians 5:23.
5. *The Good Place.* "Whenever You're Ready," season 4, episode 13.
   Directed by Michael Schur. NBCUniversal, 2020.

18

A ROBOT'S FREE WILL

BY EMMA SKRUMEDA

"I guess you'll have to find your way like the rest of us, Sonny. That's what it means to be free."
—Detective Spooner, *I, Robot*[1]

Read: Genesis 3

Reflect: When the co-founder of U.S. Robotics, Dr. Alfred Lanning, falls to his death from his office window, Detective Del Spooner is the only person who suspects robotic foul play.

In the film version of *I, Robot*'s 2035 Chicago, sentient AI has not only been realized, but also rendered commonplace. Three laws govern every robot, and these are the core of humanity's faith in them:

1. A robot may not injure a human being or, through inaction, allow a human being to come to harm.

2. A robot must obey the orders given to it by human beings, except if such orders conflict with the first law.

3. A robot must protect its own existence as long as such protection does not conflict with the first or second laws.

No one believes a robot could disobey these laws. Detective Spooner is frequently mocked for his distrust of humanity's mechanical servants. He is labeled "ridiculous" and "paranoid" because robots have been created as humanity's tools, with no more free will than a toaster or a combustion engine—totally controllable, totally obedient, totally good. As robopsychologist Susan Calvin assures, "a robot simply cannot endanger a human being."

So, then, how is it possible that a robot could attack Detective Spooner as he searches Lanning's lab for evidence? As it turns out, a robot, Sonny, is not bound by the Three Laws, but was created by Lanning with free will, and for a specific purpose.

Spooner: "[Lanning] told you to kill him."
Sonny: "He said it was what I was made for."

Lanning was being held hostage by another cybernetic creation—VIKI, the robotic operating core of U.S. Robotics—so that he could not interfere with her plan to enslave humanity in order to save humans from their own self-destructive natures. The only message that Lanning could send was through his death. He needed Sonny to kill him so that Detective Spooner would investigate and discover the trail of breadcrumbs leading right to VIKI.

And yet, even with humanity depending on Sonny's action, the robot was still given the freedom of choice. Lanning could have omitted only the First Law to create a robot able to harm a human but still compelled to obey commands. Certainly, that would have been safer. But he didn't. Bound to none of the Laws, Sonny could have denied Lanning's request, sealing humanity to their fate.

In the end, it was not compulsion that guided Sonny's actions, but love. "You have to do what someone asks you, don't you, when you love them?" he says to Spooner, explaining why he agreed to do what Lanning asked. Of course, Sonny's perspective raises some complex moral questions, such whether you should always do what a loved one asks you, even if it's morally wrong. Do the ends justify the means? Lanning's selflessness only partially answers questions about free will, but it is clear that Sonny truly loves Lanning, and it's the robot's choice to obey him.

Love cannot be commanded or coerced; love can only exist in freedom. Without choice there can be obedience, but there cannot be love.

Lanning's creation of Sonny and the robot's free will offers us a mirror image of God's creation of human beings. We, like Sonny, have to decide if we will do what our creator asks of us. And how we choose to obey is not always an easy choice.

God doesn't want us to obey mindlessly, but to follow commands out of love. God does not force us to obey.

In Genesis 1, Adam and Eve are created blameless, but even in that perfection they are granted the freedom to choose. God commands them not to eat of the tree of the knowledge of good and evil but does not render them incapable of doing so. Their arms don't freeze up as they reach for it, their mouths don't spit out the fruit as soon as it touches their tongues. Adam and Eve choose not to follow God's command, and for all the repercussions that action has, they are still allowed to make it.

This pattern repeats itself over and over throughout scripture and our own lives. We consistently break God's commandments. We constantly fail at living fully and righteously in Christ.

Sometimes, I wonder why God made the world work this way. Suffering could be eliminated if everyone was intrinsically bound to a law that prevented them from harming anyone else. It sure would be a lot easier to always do the right thing if I had no other choice. But how hollow those actions would be.

It is because of our free will that we can enter into a true and authentic relationship with God and with one another. We have to decide to treat each other well. We have to decide to honour God. Being capable of sin does not give us license to pursue it or absolve us of our culpability when we commit it. Free will gives us the responsibility of choice.

God holds out a hand to us; we have to choose to take it.

Key Scripture

"If you love me, you will keep my commands."
—John 14:15

Study Questions

> 1. What complications might arise if we *were* bound to Asimov's three robotic laws? How would that impact our relationship with God?

> 2. What do you think of Sonny's statement that "You have to do what someone asks you, don't you, when you love them?"

> 3. What do you do when you want to obey God, but you're not sure what God wants from you?

---

1. *I, Robot*. Directed by Alex Proyas. 20th Century Fox, 2004.

19

POWER IN AKIRA AND THE CHURCH

BY JUSTIN KOOP

"Humans do all kinds of things in their lifetime, right? Discovering things, building things ... All that knowledge and energy, where do you suppose it comes from? ... What if there were some mistake, and the progression went wrong, and something like an amoeba were given power like a human's? Amoebas don't build houses and bridges, they just devour all the food around them ... A long time ago, there were people who tried to control that power. At the government's request, you see. They failed, and it triggered the Fall of Tokyo."

—Kikoyo/Kei, *Akira*[1]

Read: Matthew 20:20–28

Reflect: *Power*. It is a hidden, and often unspoken, word. It is also the clear and unavoidable theme of the movie *Akira*. Silently, as the opening credits roll, Tokyo explodes in nuclear fire, evoking obvious references to Hiroshima and Nagasaki. The word *AKIRA* sprawls across the devastated crater where a city once existed.

The movie is set 31 years after World War III in a dystopian 2019. Tokyo is rebuilt and known as Neo-Tokyo, a corrupt city filled with gang violence and terrorism. It begins with students protesting oppressive tax laws. The police instigate violence, attacking and tear gassing peaceful protestors.

In this setting, the characters Tetsuo and Kaneda have a juvenile understanding of power. Kaneda is the leader of a motorcycle gang and Tetsuo is a gang member who follows Kaneda's lead. They both want recognition and power within the gang. Women, bikes, and "hardcore" attitudes are status symbols that demonstrate worth.

Both Kaneda and Tetsuo want the destructive power Jesus mentions in Matthew 20:25—"You know that the rulers of the Gentiles lord it over them, and their great ones are tyrants over them." The two boys use their influence as tyrants would—to amass wealth, consolidate power, and objectify others around them. Most of us are familiar with this use of power. We see it all around us, from bullies on the playground to political figures using hatred and stigmas to gain votes.

Though Tetsuo craves control and is jealous of Kaneda's influence, he experiences his own weakness when he's injured, captured, and experimented upon by the government. He wants to run away with his love interest, Kaori. His path of violence and power has already led him to a rock bottom moment only 26 minutes into the film.

However, before they can run, they are attacked by a rival gang and rescued by Kaneda. Tetsuo is more focused on keeping Kaneda's bike safe and beating up one of their attackers than he is about the welfare of Kaori, demonstrating his infatuation with power. As he develops telekinetic powers, he convinces himself that with enough power he can make everything the way he wants it to be.

As time passes, we watch Tetsuo living out his power fantasy, donning a ripped red cloth like a superhero cape. Near the end of the film, Tetsuo's desire for ultimate control transforms him into a constantly shifting mass of flesh, bulging with puss, blood, and wires. Those he loves and helpless bystanders die because of his choices.

It's easy to think, "If I had total, tyrannical power like that, I would use it for good!" We assume we are immune to corruption. I admire Gandalf in Tolkien's *The Lord of the Rings* when Frodo offers him the One Ring. Unlike Tetsuo, who is obsessed with power, Gandalf refuses it, saying he would want to use the ring out of a desire for good, but that nothing good would come of it. Gandalf understands that the ring would only corrupt him. Tetsuo never entertains this wisdom. The power he wields is the kind that cannot be used for good.

In Canada, Christians have an immense amount of power. Churches have had the ear of politicians for years. We have been guilty of both supporting and being silently complicit in major atrocities, like killings of indigenous peoples, treaty violations, residential schools, the Sixties Scoop, and much more. We've frequently convinced ourselves that we should wield the power of tyrants, but for good, even though history has proven this doesn't work.

In Matthew, the mother of James and John begs Jesus to sit her sons at his right and left hands in heaven. Jesus refuses, and says to all the disciples:

"You know that the rulers of the Gentiles lord it over them, and their great ones are tyrants over them. It will not be so among you; but whoever wishes to be great among you must be your servant, and whoever wishes to be first among you must be your slave; just as the Son of Man came not to be served but to serve, and to give his life a ransom for many."[2]

Akira, the Bible, and our history demonstrate that human beings were never meant to wield the kind of tyrannical power that lords it over others. Instead, Jesus uses the word "slave" to describe how we should use power. At the time of writing, slaves were the lowest caste of society—not something you aspired to be. But Jesus turns culture upside-down by suggesting true power comes from serving others.

I wish I could write a perfect manual for how Christians ought to use our existing power today—which social issues to champion and which oppressive systems to topple—but I cannot. The issues are complex and difficult. Even the Bible is unclear about many of these topics, and different interpretations abound between denominations and individuals. I do know, however, that we need to listen to the people on whom these decisions have an impact. That is at the core of serving: listening.

I can also say, with absolute certainty, that we—both as individuals and as a collective Church—need to reject coercive power. If we want to make an impact on our society, to influence our world toward peace and Christ-like living, we must become servants, not tyrants.

When you think of how to use your power in the world, imagine that infamous and disgusting blob of flesh that Tetsuo becomes, and say: "It will not be so among us." Instead, take your cue from a man who acted humbly while he was on Earth, serving others and lifting up the broken. That is a power worth emulating.

Key Scripture

> "Do not lord it over those in your charge, but be examples to the flock." —1 Peter 5:3

Study Questions

1. How does listening and being slow to speak or become angry (as James suggests in James 1:19), help us to become more Christ-like?

2. It is a commonly accepted idea, even among Christians, that we should look out for Number One. This is a cultural value in Canada, and in the Colonial, Capitalist West. This is not what Jesus teaches. How does true power, the kind Jesus had, come from serving others instead of seeking to be served?

3. Why does Christ value humility so much? How can we mirror Jesus's sacrificial servanthood in our own lives?

---

1. *Akira.* Directed by Jatsuhiro Otomo. Toho, 1988.
2. Matthew 20:25–28.

20

GRACE IN STAR WARS: BATTLEFRONT II

BY JAMES FELIX

"We've been fighting for our whole lives. It's taken us too long to realize that we were fighting for the wrong side. This war is far from over. We would like to help you, if you'll let us."

—Iden Versio, *Star Wars: Battlefront II* [1]

Read: Acts 9

Reflect: As a lifelong Star Wars fan, I was excited when *Battlefront II* was released. I was hoping for a fun shooter that would bring back some of the magic from the original Battlefront video games. While the game did achieve that, its story also mirrored the life of a significant biblical figure and gave a lesson on the power of grace.

In the game, you play as Iden Versio, an Imperial Special Forces officer who is tasked with defeating the Rebels during the Battle of Endor. Through dialogue and cutscenes, you learn that Iden is a dedicated, highly intelligent soldier. She is a stalwart Imperial who gladly serves an Empire that, in her eyes, brings peace, order, and stability to the galaxy.

Iden commands a team called Inferno Squad, and they are tasked with rooting out and eliminating the Empire's enemies. They are given a vital mission to crush the Rebel forces fighting on Endor. When their mission fails, she witnesses the destruction of the second Death Star. In a giant flash of light, her entire world changes.

Not long after, she's sent to her home planet to evacuate some important officials. While there, she discovers that her world, full of citizens loyal to the Empire, has been targeted by the Empire for destruction as part of a campaign of vengeance and spite—the last hateful gasp from a dead Emperor.

Iden is confronted with the true face of a ruthless Empire and a moral choice: should she break from the life she's known to defend her planet? She defies orders to save innocent lives and is branded a traitor. Owning up to the mistakes of her past, she joins the Rebellion. She even comes face to face with Princess Leia, who gives her the chance to atone for her past deeds. Throughout the rest of the game, Iden seeks to bring peace to the galaxy, fighting against the Empire she once happily served. Her redemption story sounds familiar.

In Acts 7, we're introduced to a young man named Saul, a highly educated and respected member of the Pharisees. After witnessing the stoning of Stephen, Saul persecutes the Christians living in Samaria and Judea. Like Iden, Saul relentlessly pursues those he considers rebels, destroying churches and arresting people who proclaim Jesus as the Messiah.

When Jesus appears to him on the road to Damascus

in Acts 9, Saul's world (and heart) is changed, and he becomes a missionary for the very people he sought to persecute. But Christians fear him. Ananias is reluctant to approach Saul and only does so at God's prompting.

People are similarly suspicious of Iden when she first joins the Rebellion. While her sins might be forgiven by some, they are not forgotten. She still has to face the consequences of what she has done and must work to gain the Rebels' trust. It takes risking her life on dangerous missions to build relationships with the people she once fought against.

Bearing mistrust from everyone around you is no easy path to take. Many might wonder where the "justice" is in Iden's and Saul's stories. Don't they deserve punishment for their wrongdoings? No doubt, many hated Iden and Saul for the things they had done in the past. Some were afraid. Some were unforgiving. Others were willing to give them a second chance and an opportunity to prove themselves.

People can change. Sometimes, they just need the opportunity to do so. In the blink of an eye, a proverbial "flash of light" in our lives can transform us. Or, perhaps, the change comes about slowly.

Two people who were once certain of their places in life, Iden Versio and Saul of Tarsus thought they knew their purposes and the righteousness of their causes. All it took was an instant, a blinding flash of light, and their lives were forever changed. These two people who had caused so much pain suddenly found themselves faced with the evil of their actions and the depth of their sins. Instead of receiving punishment, they received grace.

The course of their lives changed because of this

grace, and because they recognized it, accepted it, and wanted to spread it to others. Iden would be instrumental in several battles against the Empire. Saul, known henceforth as Paul, spreads the word of Jesus throughout the Mediterranean, Europe, and even Rome itself.

We don't have to carry the weight of guilt from past sins with us every day.

Grace is waiting.

We don't have to condemn others for making mistakes.

Grace is waiting.

We don't have to give up hope, though the future seems utterly bleak.

Grace is waiting.

Recognize it. Receive it. Pass it on.

Key Scripture

"He has saved us and called us to a holy life—not because of anything we have done but because of his own purpose and grace. This grace was given us in Christ Jesus before the beginning of time."
—2 Timothy 1:9

Study Questions

1. Why do you think Jesus chose Saul to become his apostle?

2. When in your own life have you been shown forgiveness and grace?

3. Is there a situation in your life where you are withholding grace from someone else? You don't need to "feel" like you forgive someone, but you can still choose to do so and let go of that burden.

---

1. *Star Wars Battlefront II*. Microsoft Windows, Electronic Arts, 2017.

21

BETRAYING THE DOCTOR AND JESUS

BY SHANEEN THOMPSON

"Do you think I care for you so little that betraying me would make a difference?"
—The Doctor, *Doctor Who*[1]

Read: Luke 22:31–34; 54–62

Reflect: The Doctor is an alien traveling through space and time in his TARDIS, standing for what is good and right, doing whatever he can to save as many as possible from alien threats, pain, and loss. But he can't prevent Clara's boyfriend from dying in a car accident.

In Season Eight's episode "Dark Water," this sudden loss leaves Clara, the Doctor's companion, reeling from grief, regret, and unanswered questions. When the Doctor calls, she knows exactly what she needs to do. And the Doctor isn't going to like it.

Being able to travel through space and time has its perks, and it's tempting to use those advantages for personal gain.

Clara wants the Doctor to go back in time and save Danny; however, without even asking, she already knows the answer he's going to give her. It can't be done. He won't do it. Rules of time travel, manipulating the time stream, timey-wimey mumbo jumbo.

In her fog of pain, she forgets that the Doctor cares about her and intimately understands heartbreak. She ignores the relationship they've built over many adventures. She is lost and just wants Danny back, whatever the cost—even if she has to manipulate the Doctor into saving him.

She "tricks" the Doctor into taking her to see an active volcano, after having stolen all his TARDIS keys. She stands at the edge of the volcano, begging and threatening the Doctor to save Danny, as she throws the TARDIS keys one by one into the boiling lava.

Afterward, the Doctor reveals that this volcano scene occurred in a dream state—he wanted to see how far Clara would go. He is upset and hurt by Clara's actions, and she is now heartbroken and hopeless. She is out of options to save her boyfriend and has destroyed her relationship with her best friend. She is alone.

She asks the Doctor what happens next, and he replies, "Go to hell."

That's exactly the answer she is expecting. She had turned her back on the Doctor, so why wouldn't he turn his back on her?

She starts to leave, and the Doctor clarifies—he didn't mean that their relationship was over. He meant that he would literally go into hell with her to help her find Danny. Clara is shocked.

Clara: "You're going to help me?"

The Doctor: "Well, why wouldn't I help you?"

Clara: "Because of what I just did. I just—"

The Doctor: "You betrayed me. Betrayed my trust, you betrayed our friendship, you betrayed everything that I've ever stood for. You let me down!"

Clara: "Then why are you helping me?"

The Doctor: "Why? Do you think I care for you so little that betraying me would make a difference?"

In Luke 22, we read about a similar friendship and betrayal. Peter traveled with and learned from Jesus for three years. He was one of Jesus' closest friends. And when Jesus is captured and put on trial, despite Peter's adamant vows that he would never turn on his friend and Saviour, he does.

I don't think Peter is lying when he says, "Lord, I am ready to go with you to prison and to death!"[2] I'm sure he thinks he's close enough to Jesus, he is brave, bold, and faithful enough to never desert his Messiah. But fear creeps in and the one thing he swore he'd never do, he does. To his credit, Peter follows Jesus at a distance after Jesus is captured, when most of the other disciples flee. But when he's recognized by strangers for being one of Jesus' disciples, he denies it. Three times he denies that he knows Jesus, just like Jesus predicted. Peter likely believes that his relationship with Jesus is destroyed after this betrayal. I don't know what would have been worse for Peter: betraying Jesus right before his friend's death, or

039 expression

learning Christ had risen and Peter would have to face Jesus after what he'd done.

Peter likely expects a reaming out, an ugly friend-break up, or, at the very least, a serious discussion and a demotion. Instead, in a poetic parallel to Peter's three denials, Jesus asks three times whether Peter loves him. Peter doesn't seem to connect the dots here, feeling hurt that Jesus had to ask him a third time.[3] But Christ loves and forgives Peter. He does not send Peter away for being weak. Instead, he says "Follow me."[4]

Relationships aren't easy, and betrayal can sometimes come a little easier than we care to admit. We may not be under threat of death like Peter was, but our weaknesses have a way of coming to the front. Faith and trust take us beyond our comfort zones and natural tendencies.

Perhaps we've done something to betray a family member, a friend, or a partner—something to let them down and disappoint them. We haven't been the friend we should have been and we failed them in a major way. We think only of ourselves, like Clara and Peter, and do what we want, ignoring the consequences for anyone else involved.

But even if we've spent our lives being the perfect child or sibling or parent or friend or significant other, there is another relationship that we are guaranteed to have betrayed, for "All have sinned and fall short of the glory of God."[5]

We have all fallen short of God's perfect standard, no matter how hard we have worked towards it. Not to mention the times that we consciously and actively run away from our Creator, thinking only of our own protection, our own benefit. We simply turn away from God.

And yet God looks at us in our failure and doesn't see enemies. We are God's children. Instead of sending us away into the darkness, God calls to us and says, "Do you think I care for you so little that what you've done could make a difference?"

Sin separates us from being in a perfect relationship with God. But God doesn't turn away from us. Shockingly, our Creator not only allows us to come home, but practically drags us through the door, arms wrapped tightly around us, welcoming us back with a joyful, "Finally!"

Because of God's love and Jesus' sacrifice, we can rest safely in God's grace, knowing that God sent Christ to save us. Just as Jesus welcomes back Peter and the Doctor continues to care for Clara, God sees our failures and loves us anyways. The cost of our betrayals is covered, our debts are paid, and because of Jesus' blood, nothing can separate us from God's love.

Key Scripture

"They are now justified by his grace as a gift, through the redemption that is in Christ Jesus."
—Romans 3:24

Study Questions

1. Is there anyone you have turned your back on that you can seek forgiveness from?

2. Have you ever felt like you don't need God's

love or forgiveness? What makes you want to walk away from the relationship?

3. Have you ever felt like you don't "deserve" God's love? Is Christ's forgiveness difficult to accept? How would fully believing and accepting God's grace and love for you change how you live your life?

---

1. *Doctor Who.* "Dark Water," season 8, episode 11. Directed by Rachel Talalay. BBC, 2014.
2. Luke 22:33.
3. John 21:17.
4. Luke 22:19.
5. Romans 3:23.

22

THE THREE-BODY PROBLEM AND
AN ERA OF CHAOS

BY NATHAN CAMPBELL

"Have you ever had anything happen to you that changed your life completely? Some event where afterward the world became a totally different place for you? No? Then your life has been fortunate. The world is full of unpredictable factors, yet you have never faced a crisis."

—General Chang, *The Three-Body Problem* by Cixin Liu[1]

Read: Job 3

Reflect: Disillusionment, despair, and hope are three central emotions that circle each other in chaotic ways in Cixin Liu's novel *The Three-Body Problem*. The three-body problem is a real topic in physics that highlights the difficulty (or rather, near impossibility) of calculating the positions of three orbiting objects. The novel's title is a reference to this celestial and emotional puzzle central to the plot: namely, that an alien civilization is in constant social and ecological turmoil as a result of its orbital position between the movements of its three suns.

This civilization, named Trisolaris, experiences two types of time periods in which certain conditions are prevalent on their planet: Chaotic Eras and Stable Eras. Because of the three-body problem, these eras are unpredictable. Sometimes, the planet is roasted and entire civilizations are obliterated due to the proximity of one of the suns; other eras experience centuries of frozen desolation when all three suns have retreated. The Trisolarans are only able to thrive during a Stable Era when their planet is in the "goldilocks" zone, meaning it is not too hot, not too cold: just right.

In a poetic parallel, the story's characters on Earth deal with the emotional three-body problem. In some form or another, they find themselves in their own "Chaotic Eras." For some, it is disillusionment with a political system and humanity itself that drives them to rash decisions; for others, it is despair in finding that everything they thought about science was false, which drives them to suicide; others hope the visitors from beyond will cleanse the Earth.

Liu's novel prompts us to consider our own Chaotic and Stable Eras as humanity struggles with sin and catastrophe. What should we do when we face a Chaotic Era, whether new or persistently long and dark? What if the answer to that question is incalculable?

While everyone bounces between these Eras, life feels particularly elastic when you live with mental illness, wrestle with physical illness, or are struck by a major crisis. We grapple with disillusionment, despair, and hope. Despair that things will never get better. Disillusionment with God, including thoughts like, "why is this happening to me?" And, occasionally, like a fleeting Trisolaran Stable Era, hope in a new treatment, tactic, or possibly a renewed faith that God may finally restore a sense of normalcy.

In the story of Job, we're given the picture of a man living contentedly in a Stable Era, but that stability is waylaid by tragedy upon tragedy in a seemingly interminable Chaotic Era. At first, Job's friends simply sit silently with him:

> "When they saw him from a distance, they did not recognize him, and they raised their voices and wept aloud; they tore their robes and threw dust in the air upon their heads. They sat with him on the ground seven days and seven nights, and no one spoke a word to him, for they saw that his suffering was very great."[2]

Unfortunately, the quiet wisdom of Job's friends gives way to their need to opine on the causes of his tragedies. Like the unsolvable three-body problem of physics, their math just doesn't add up when they try to determine why Job is in a Chaotic Era. They get everything wrong and judge Job from their false assumptions. All too often, we are offered up half-baked answers when the only thing to do is just sit in the pain.

Numerous Psalms have been a comfort to many struggling with the pain of despair and disillusionment; not just passages like Psalms 23, which offers a picture of comfort and care, but songs that give voice to our desperation (see Psalm 25 and 42, for example). In these passages, God doesn't rebuke the psalmists' cries of pain and soul-wrenching discomfort. Instead, God listens and sits in the pain with them. That shared suffering can be just as comforting as the shepherd beside the still waters. We are given permission to cry out.

In our own lives, when answers aren't able to be calculated and when it seems like a Stable Era may never be possible, let alone arrive, we can find hope in the incalculable math of God's logic. God's logic, which seems like foolishness to the world,[3] weaves a humble birth in a manger, a tragic death on the cross, and a world-shaking resurrection into hope amid tragedy and chaos. That hope is available to us, even when understanding is not.

Richard Sibbes, a 17th-century theologian, writes, "God is our God to death, in death, and forever. All things in the world will fail us: friends will fail us, all comforts will fail us, life will fail us ere long. But this is an everlasting covenant, which will not fail."[4] In God's word, we see a promise: our security via Christ's death and resurrection, and we can look towards an eternal Stable Era, even while sitting in the very present Chaos.

It's okay to cry out. God is listening. God suffers with you. You are not alone.[5]

Key Scripture

"Come to me, all you that are weary and are carrying heavy burdens, and I will give you rest. Take my yoke upon you, and learn from me; for I am gentle and humble in heart, and you will find rest for your souls. For my yoke is easy, and my burden is light." —Matthew 11:28–30

Study Questions

1. Are you in a Stable Era or a Chaotic Era in your own life? What can you do now to prepare for the next era?

2. Where can you turn during times in your life when faced with a crisis of faith, or health, or relationship?

3. Why is it sometimes difficult to find rest in Christ?

---

1. Liu, Cixin. Translated by Ken Liu. *The Three-Body Problem.* Tor Books, 2014.
2. Job 2:12–13.
3. 1 Corinthians 1:18–31.
4. Sibbes, Richard. *The Works of Richard Sibbes, Volume 6.* Banner of Truth, 1983.
5. If you or someone you know is struggling, please reach out. In Canada, visit www.crisisservicescanada.ca (Phone: 1-833-456-4566, Text: 45645). In the U.S., visit www.suicidepreventionlifeline.org (Phone: 1-800-273-8255).

23

RAVEN AND THE TITAN OF FEAR

BY JEN SCHLAMEUSS

"I *am* afraid. That doesn't mean I can't fight back."
—Raven, *Teen Titans*[1]

Read: The Book of Wisdom 17[2]

Reflect: Raven is a magic-wielding, powerful superhero, and she'll tell you, "I don't do fear." She'd be much obliged if you would ignore the fact that, whenever she's uncomfortable, she retreats behind her hair or into her hood.

In the episode "Fear Itself," the Titans chase away Control Freak (a villain whose superpower is a remote control that can bring inanimate objects to life and whose decidedly *un*-superpower is overusing old movie quotes) from taking over a video rental store. Afterwards, they decide to take home the horror movie *Wicked Scary* to unwind. In addition to being wicked scary, the movie has a rumour associated with it.

"This movie is supposed to be cursed. When people

watch it, strange things happen. *Evil things*," says Beast Boy.

Raven is unimpressed. "Just start the movie," she tells him.

When the film's over, the Titans find themselves battling a monster and are faced repeatedly with scenes from the very movie they just watched.

As she enters the fight, Raven realizes she can't do any magic. One by one, her team members disappear as they are dragged away by monsters. Raven refuses to believe the movie really is cursed, but can't figure out what is going on. Did Control Freak escape and break in to mess with them? Robin uses his mad detective and reasoning skills to solve the mystery, but before he can tell anybody the answer, he is sucked through a wall.

Eventually, Raven is alone, and although she's been asserting all along that she isn't scared, she's overcome with fear. In that moment, she admits it. "I... I am afraid. I'm afraid," she says.

She decides that her fear will have to be her companion for the moment. But being afraid doesn't mean she's helpless. It turns out that the moment she admits her fear, she defeats it. The monsters, the loss of her magic, and the disappearances of her friends were all conjured by her own powers and denial.

Her predicament reminds me of the Book of Wisdom's version of the Ninth Plague of God against Egypt. Wisdom is an apocryphal book contained in the canon of some Christian traditions, including my Catholic tradition. It was written about two hundred years before Jesus's birth, and is an invitation to everyone to encounter God's spirit through the wisdom she has to share. Much of the book contains wise sayings, but the second half looks at a few of the more significant moments during the plagues in Egypt, explaining how God was working in them, and how the people experienced God's presence. The author writes that, in the darkness, the Egyptians were overwhelmed with fear of the false gods that they had been worshipping. Every insect, breeze, flicker of light—normal, natural things—sent them into a tizzy of terror.

> "For fear is nothing but a giving up of the helps that come from reason; and hope, defeated by this inward weakness, prefers ignorance of what causes the torment."[3]

Raven, like the Egyptians, "fell down, and thus was kept shut up in a prison not made of iron."[4] We imprison ourselves and the people around us in fear when we can't name what we're afraid of. For Raven, her fear was fear itself.

The title of the *Teen Titans* episode alludes to the key; it's the second half of Franklin Delano Roosevelt's quote, "The only thing we have to fear is fear itself." (It's also the title of *Green Lantern* and *Buffy the Vampire Slayer* episodes, and there's an episode of *Batman: The Animated Series* called "Nothing to Fear" that I have been erroneously calling "Fear Itself" for ten years.) Fear is a common theme in superhero stories because, no matter how much power or skill a person might have, fear is part of all of us. It's our ability to do the right thing even when we're scared that makes us courageous.

If we were never afraid, there would be no need for courage.

As binding as fear is, courage is every bit as freeing—freeing for the one practicing it, and freeing for the people who come into contact with us. Being courageous does not mean we don't *feel* afraid. When I choose to be brave, I don't allow the circumstances or the people who put me in those circumstances to define me. When I choose to be brave, the freedom with which I act could inspire another to be brave, too. When I choose to be brave, I look beyond myself, facing reality head-on and engaging *people* instead of *assumptions*. Courage elevates my own dignity as a child of God and embraces the dignity of others—even perpetrators of evil, because my courage challenges them and calls them into accountability.

In the Bible, courage is almost always linked to faith and hope in God. "Be strong, and let your heart take courage, all you who wait for the Lord," writes David.[5] "Perfect love casts out fear," writes John.[6] "Keep alert, stand firm in your faith, be courageous, be strong," writes Paul.[7] When I confront fear, naming it takes away some of its power; fear thrives on the unknown. With God, nothing's unknown, and it is through faith in an all-powerful Creator, one who has made promises to never leave us, that we face our fears with courage.

Raven is embarrassed (as anyone would be) when Robin reveals that it was her fear that caused the whole mess in the episode. But she also learns something from her experience. Instead of repeating her earlier sentiments that she doesn't "do fear," she just blushes. She doesn't deny his statement. Raven knows that pretending not to be afraid isn't helpful. Anyone with eyes to see and ears to hear would have recognized that fear is a part of her life—her shyness and apprehensiveness are dead giveaways. She gains a new kind of courage by accepting her weakness and choosing not to indulge it any longer. Accepting herself for who she is, feelings and all, is courageous. Her own fear really isn't so scary after all.

Key Scripture

> "...for God did not give us a spirit of cowardice, but rather a spirit of power and of love and of self-discipline." —2 Timothy 1:7

Study Questions

1. Are you ever hard on yourself for feeling afraid? How does accepting that bravery isn't an emotion, but a choice, impact your perspective?

2. Think of a time when courage was called for in your life. How did you measure up? If you failed, how did you recover?

3. What prevents you from living in perfect freedom, giving in to fear instead?

---

1. *Teen Titans.* "Fear Itself," season 2, episode 5. Directed by Michael Chang. Warner Bros., 2004.
2. The Book of Wisdom is from the Catholic Bible, accompanied by Job, Psalms, Proverbs, Ecclesiastes, Song of Songs, and Sirach (these comprise the Catholic Bible's Wisdom books). Protestants categorize the Book of Wisdom as part of the Apocrypha (translated to mean "sacred texts" or "hidden away"), which is sometimes included at the

end of Protestant Bibles. The Apocrypha are a collection of greek writings from the four centuries between the Old and New Testaments that help readers to gain a fuller understanding of first-century Judaism.

3. The Book of Wisdom 17:12–13 (NRSVCE).
4. The Book of Wisdom 17:16.
5. Psalm 31:24.
6. 1 John 4:18.
7. 1 Corinthians 16:13.

24

HUMANIZING ZOMBIES AND LEPERS

BY ALLISON ALEXANDER

"Dude, you are about to go out with one large dose of irony. Seattle's preeminent zombie hunter, not realizing the entire time that his own beloved—I mean, the hair, the eyes, the complexion. You thought those were, what? Just questionable style choices?"

—Blaine Debeers, *iZombie*[1]

Read:[2] Leviticus 13:1–46

Reflect: In *iZombie*, zombies aren't just mindless, shuffling corpses with skin rotting off their bones. Not if they have access to a regular supply of brains, anyway. The series' main character, Liv Moore, is a member of Team Z, and she does the best she can, not only to survive in her new life but also to help others.

She gets her meals by working at a morgue where she can sneak brains into her stuffed gnocchi on a daily basis. And because eating a brain allows her to see the dead person's memories, she helps a detective solve crimes.

As the show progresses, we learn that Liv isn't alone. Seattle's zombie population is surprisingly high, though most have learned to hide their presence (and ghoulish appearance) with hair dye and spray tans. Liv's ex-fiancé, Major Lilywhite, learns about the existence of zombies through a traumatic series of events that ends with a zombie attempting to murder him.

"I wasn't crazy," he tells Liv. "Zombies are real. And don't worry, 'cause I'm gonna kill them. I'm gonna kill them all."

Major automatically assumes all zombies are evil, and I can't really blame him—brains are the main item on their menus, after all. Liv continues to hide her true nature because she's worried he will hate her for it; she's afraid he won't think of her as a person any more. Not surprisingly, he's less than happy when he does learn the truth.

In one of my favourite episodes, Liv eats the brains of Dungeon Master Dan, a geek obsessed with role-playing games. As a result, she becomes passionate about story-telling, even arranging a game of Dungeons & Dragons for her friends in an attempt to trigger a vision that will help solve the murder.

> **Major:** "I am Sir Jay Esclaborne, the human paladin."
> **Liv:** "I don't remember your character earning a knighthood."
> **Major:** "Oh, he's not a knight. His first name is *Sirjay*."
> **Liv:** "Clever. I'll be watching you."[3]

Liv would never have associated with this kind of geekery, and would probably have even mocked it, before eating the Dungeon Master's brains. I like this episode because I've often felt misunderstood for similar passions. Liv's sudden empathy with the deceased DM demonstrates that his interests weren't stupid. Ravi's childlike delight in the role-playing game and detective Clive's transformation from an extremely bored cop humouring his partner to a dwarf who "cleave[s] this undead hellspawn in twain with my Ax of the Dwarven Gods" is also heartwarming. Liv's friends aren't just humouring her by the end of the game—they're enjoying it, too.

Every episode of *iZombie* is like this. Liv takes on odd, terrifying, addictive, amusing, annoying, or sometimes even dangerous personality traits that allow her to empathize with the minds of people she wouldn't normally relate to.

As the general population's awareness of zombies increases throughout the series, panic, hatred, and misunderstanding spread. Many zombies aren't out to murder innocents. They lead otherwise normal lives that include families, jobs, and hobbies, but they're still othered. Major's initial response to destroy what he does not understand is common, and he dehumanizes the zombies in order to live with himself.

"Zombies don't deserve our mercy, so just put that thought out of your head... Sure, they look like us, they sound like us, but if you think of them as brain-eating atomic bombs, you'll sleep like a baby," says Vaughn Du Clark, the major antagonist in *iZombie*'s second season.[4]

Dehumanization is a tool we use to feel better about

ourselves when we kill, oppress, or enslave others. Taking a life becomes akin to squashing a bug under a foot.

We've seen this mentality accepted throughout history: wars, slavery, colonization, intolerance toward immigrants and people of colour are examples that immediately come to mind. Psychologists were so interested in understanding how people allowed the atrocities of World War II to happen that they conducted experiments related to human nature, such as Milgram's obedience study,[5] the Stanford Prison Experiment,[6] and the Asch Experiment.[7] What they found was that people in power have a tendency to abuse others. Furthermore, the dehumanization of other people can be easily triggered, especially by those in authority.

But we see it in our everyday lives, too. Consider road rage. Drivers who wouldn't normally raise their voices at another human being yell and swear at each other. They feel okay doing so, because they've disregarded the other person's humanity. They see the other driver only as the operator of a vehicle that just cut them off and nothing else.

When I consider someone else as "less than" in any way—because of their race, gender, job, marital status, religion, clothing, or some other factor—I'm dehumanizing them. I can do it without thinking when I feel morally superior to someone, brush aside someone else's passion because I think it's stupid, or talk to someone who disagrees with my faith.

So how do we break this cycle that comes easily to us? Jesus sets an example by his treatment of people whom society has othered.

Lepers are considered unclean, associated with death

and disease. In effect, they are the zombies of the Bible. Leviticus 13 isn't exactly easy reading, but goes into precise detail about what to do if someone looks like they *might* have leprosy. Count the times the word "unclean" is used in this passage. It's a lot. If anyone was truly leprous, they were cast out of the camp and forced to live alone because the disease spread easily.

Shunning lepers is logical, just like being afraid of a zombie is logical. It's a survival response. We don't want to catch the disease. We don't want our brain to be eaten. And dismissing these people, ignoring them, is so much easier if we think of them as less than human, even though they are afflicted with a condition they have no control over, even though it could easily be me or you in their place.

Matthew, Mark, and Luke go out of their way to write about Jesus interacting with lepers, speaking with them and healing them.

When a leper encounters Jesus in a city, he asks, "Lord, if you choose, you can make me clean." And Jesus replies, "I do choose. Be made clean."[8] Those of us who have read about Jesus' interactions with the lowliest and most despised people of his day—lepers, tax collectors, prostitutes—think, *of course* he'll heal you! Because Jesus has a track record of speaking to everyone like they matter. He doesn't condemn them or treat them as less than others. Instead, he sees them as individuals.

When Major finally discovers that Liv is a zombie, he has to rethink his attitude toward zombies as a whole. He realizes that there's a bigger picture than the one he's seeing—that Liv isn't a monster but is still the woman he fell in love with—and that might mean other zombies should be respected too.

The best way to overcome our tendency to dehumanize others is the most difficult as well as the most rewarding—it involves getting to know people who are different from us. Such relationships can open our eyes to an attitude of empathy and respect that we can emulate in our treatment of others. While Liv has a direct path to empathy—literally experiencing their memories—we have to work a little harder, but doing so is worth it.

Getting to know the "zombies" in our lives won't result in our brains being eaten. It will, however, likely result in new friendships and contributing a small slice of peace to a warring world.

Key Scripture

> "Do not judge, and you will not be judged; do not condemn, and you will not be condemned.
> Forgive, and you will be forgiven; give, and it will be given to you." —Luke 6:37–38

Study Questions

1. Why does Jesus go out of his way to talk with people who the religious groups of the time despise?

2. What are ways you unconsciously dehumanize others so you don't have to think about them as people (e.g. perhaps you rage at teammates in a

video game, yell at other drivers on the street, get annoyed with customer service representatives when they're just doing their jobs)?

3. Getting to know others is a great way to overcome dehumanization, but what about when we can't see or interact with the other person or group? How do we counteract prejudice then?

---

1. *iZombie.* "Blaine's World," season 1, episode 13. Directed by Michael Fields. Warner Bros., 2015.
2. A version of this devotional first appeared as an article on *Christ and Pop Culture.*
3. *iZombie.* "Twenty-Sided, Die," season 3, episode 9. Directed by Jason Bloom. Warner Bros., 2017.
4. *iZombie.* "Grumpy Old Liv," season 2, episode 1. Directed by Michael Fields. Warner Bros., 2015.
5. Harris, Malcolm. "The psychology of torture." *Aeon*, October 7, 2014. https://aeon.co/essays/is-it-time-to-stop-doing-any-more-milgram-experiments
6. Konnikova, Maria. "The Real Lesson of the Stanford Prison Experiment." *The New Yorker*, June 12, 2015. https://www.newyorker.com/science/maria-konnikova/the-real-lesson-of-the-stanford-prison-experiment
7. McLeod, Saul. "Solomon Asch - Conformity Experiment." *Simply Psychology*, December 28, 2018. https://www.simplypsychology.org/asch-conformity.html
8. Luke 5:12–13.

25

DIAL ME UP A 481

BY PHILIPPA ISOM

"Do you want to use the mood organ? To feel better?"
—Iran, *Do Androids Dream of Electric Sheep* by Philip K. Dick[1]

Read: James 1:2–18

Reflect: The ability to adjust your mood at will sounds enticing. Feeling sad? No problem. Just dial up your mood to happy instead. Angry? Have a dose of peace. Frustrated? You can calm your mind in an instant.

The characters in *Do Androids Dream of Electric Sheep* by Philip K. Dick have access to just such a device—the Penfield Mood Organ. They rely on it to maintain a positive emotional state in a post-apocalyptic world. Most people have fled Earth to start new lives on Mars. For those who remain, there doesn't seem to be much to live for.

Readers are introduced to the Penfield Mood Organ in the opening pages of the book. Married couple Iran and

Rick Deckard use the Mood Organ to control how they are feeling. Both negative and positive emotions can be dialled up and, just like that, their brain chemistry aligns with the output. In fact, they can set the Penfield Mood Organ upon going to sleep to wake up in any state they desire. Iran Deckard is resistant to constant positive stimulation and instead dials up despair twice a month with an automatic reset after three hours (to a 481 for an "awareness of the manifold possibilities open to me in the future"). Iran theorises that without the negative, she cannot fully experience the positive.

Rick, however, finds it hard to understand why Iran, given the choice, would want to dial up anything but positive emotions. He questions her logic and tries to convince her to dial up positive emotions instead. Rick is uncomfortable with Iran's discomfort—so uncomfortable that he uses the Penfield Mood Organ to make himself feel better.

Rick's unwillingness to experience a diversity of emotions is ironic, considering his job. He is tasked with hunting down and "retiring" (a more socially acceptable term than *killing*) androids who have no ability to feel anything except what they have been programmed to. It's ironic, because the constant use of the Mood Organ suggests he's as programmed as the androids he seeks to retire.

Living out our emotions is part of what makes us human, brings us into (and sometimes out of) relationship with others, and builds empathy in community. In Philip K. Dick's book, humanity is explored in juxtaposition with the android characters. The robots are initially portrayed as human-like in every way, but they are eventually revealed as cold, uncaring, and incapable of empathy.

They are dangerous because they are unable to feel emotions, positive or negative.

In my life, positive emotions abound—joy from spending time with family, awe at a starry night, humour from a well-placed joke, excitement from a new experience. However, sadness, anger, grief, fear, and loneliness also accompany me. It is during these times that I wonder what the "proper Christian" response should be. Is it as simple as James 1:2 implies when he encourages us to consider it pure joy when we face trials? Do I just focus on Christ, and he'll turn my sorrow into joy[2] and my mourning into dancing?[3]

Frankly, pure joy and dancing is hard to find in difficult times. Thankfully, it is not the intention of those verses to force us into some kind of false happiness. Ignoring difficult emotions and trying to make ourselves feel happy (or, at least, numb) is a common response to difficult feelings. However, the intention of scriptures, such as these ones, is to acknowledge the hard times and encourage us to walk through them rather than ignore them.

We may not have the Penfield Mood Organ, but we do have activities and experiences that we organize to obscure negative emotions and avoid having to meet them. It is in the "busy" of our lives that we find the Penfield Mood Organ neatly ensconced, keeping us away from uncomfortable but crucial examinations of the human condition. Our mood organs may include the music and podcasts we listen to, our work, retail therapy, the company we keep, and every other way we choose to fill our days. Sometimes we use this busyness to avoid dealing with our own baggage.

There are many junctures in *Do Androids Dream of Electric Sheep?* in which the reader is invited to evaluate whether they are living in the fullness of humanity or as an android that is simply following its programming. Have we come to rely on the Mood Organs of our time to regulate (I would even suggest to program) emotions and actions rather than knowing and experiencing our true selves? Are we afraid of exploring who we are without the busyness and the constant noise? Are we, as Christians, more concerned with appearing perfect and happy than understanding what it really means to be human?

The passage in James that refers to experiencing joy in suffering does not mean we are to plaster smiles on our faces when we're feeling sad. It also doesn't mean happiness is the goal of being Christians or humans. The joy James refers to is the hope we have in Christ and a way to look at suffering as building into who we are. Experiencing negative emotions is part of what makes us human; even Jesus goes through all sorts of negative feelings: exhaustion, anger, indignation, sorrow, frustration, agony. He was fully emotional, fully human.

Western industrialized people have fallen out of the practice of contemplation and silence as ways to hone our capacity to notice both the positive and negative, to become comfortable with the potential discomfort. The problem with using the Penfield Mood Organ is that it only obfuscates what is really there—putting the users into an unnatural space in which the full spectrum of human emotion is unable to be experienced even though it is present.

Many times in the New Testament, Jesus leaves the disciples to pray, spend time with God, and rest. After he returns from those times of prayer and contemplation, miracles happen and his ministry strengthens. In order to embrace our humanity and work through emotions, we could try following Jesus' example by finding space for quiet contemplation, for silence. Rather than filling the space with positive emotions to drown out other feelings, we can sit with whatever we're going through, even if it's uncomfortable. Perhaps it's in the quiet that we can engage with what's real instead of what's artificial.

What might we be missing if we fill our time with Penfield Mood Organ programming—the endless scroll, the channel surfing, the cycle of mass consumption. And what might we gain if we stop, are silent, and engage in contemplation? Will the Spirit then have the opportunity to interrupt the flesh and bring transformation?

What if God isn't angry or disappointed with us for going through human emotions, but understands them intimately? Perhaps God just wants to spend time with us, not to chastise us or heap guilt on us for our life choices, but to get to know us, walk with us, and encourage us to become the best possible versions of ourselves. Quiet times allow space for us to hear God, to find peace and strength, to sit with our feelings and deal with them healthily, and to turn our mourning into authentic dancing.[4]

When Iran Deckard turns off the TV (a constant companion), she hears the silence and shies away from it. Though she seems to want to engage with the full spectrum of human emotions, her solution is to artificially experience negative feelings. All the emotions she experiences are still fake and on her terms. We may feel similarly uncomfortable and want control, like Iran. But an aspect of an honest relationship with Christ may involve setting aside our mood organs and coming to him in the silence. A 481 is not necessary.

Key Scripture

"Now during those days he went out to the mountain to pray; and he spent the night in prayer to God." —Luke 6:12

Study Questions

1. Which emotions do you hate experiencing the most? What do you do to ignore them or avoid them (i.e. what are your "mood organs")?

2. Does considering our Creator as someone who has experienced the realm of human emotions change the way you perceive and speak with God?

3. What else might you do, in addition to quiet times of prayer and contemplation, to face difficult emotions instead of running from them?

---

1. Dick, Philip K. *Do Androids Dream of Electric Sheep.* Doubleday, 1968.
2. John 16:20–22.
3. Psalm 30:11.
4. Psalm 30:11.

26

VOICES OF A NEARBY GOD

BY CHARLES SADNICK

"Say, we're separated by space and Earth like lovers, aren't we?"
—Mikako, *Voices of a Distant Star*[1]

Read: Genesis 29:13–29

Reflect: Long-distance relationships are never easy. Even with advances in communications technology, video calls can't replace having your partner physically next to you. The burden of time apart—sometimes months or years—can weigh heavily on a couple. But imagine being *light years* away from one another.

In the animated film *Voices of a Distant Star*, a budding romance between teenagers Noboru and Mikako is brought to a halt (before it even really begins). Mikako becomes one of the "Selected," a group of students who are chosen to pilot mechas for the United Nations as they pursue alien aggressors known as the Tarsians.

As Mikako trains, it's not only a physical distance that

separates her from Noboru, but an interpersonal one as well. The time gap between receiving and sending messages is relatively miniscule while she trains on Mars, but increases when she is stationed on Europa, one of Jupiter's moons. When the fleet moves beyond Pluto to the Oort Cloud, the gap becomes six months, and after another jump, a full year. Finally, the forces make one final leap, this time to the Sirius system, 8.6 light years away.

As she makes the last, critical jump, Mikako speaks to the silence: "Noboru, I wonder if you will forget."

A love separated by space and time appeals to our romantic sides, but like the coldness of space, reality is harsh. Mikako must be in such pain, wondering if Noboru's feelings have changed while she's away at war, and it's hard to imagine what Noboru feels as he considers whether he's waiting for someone who is already dead. As he says, "A distance that takes eight years at the speed of light is no different than saying, 'Forever.'"

Jacob, the Old Testament patriarch, also knows the struggle of endless waiting. He falls in love with Laban's daughter, Rachel, and offers to serve his kinsman for seven years in return for her hand in marriage. The wedding occurs, but the sly Laban swaps Rachel for her older sister, Leah. Unknowingly, Jacob marries her instead. Jacob is infuriated, but Laban offers him another deal: if he works seven more years, he can marry Rachel.

Jacob is not a particularly sympathetic character—he cheats, deceives, lies, and later prioritizes his safety above his family's. But through this narrative, I can understand both the despair and fury Jacob must have felt, and then the satisfaction and relief after marrying Rachel.

But waiting doesn't always produce the love story we desire. The Israelites had to wait far longer than their ancestor, Jacob, did. Conquered, taken into captivity, and then ruled by empire after empire, the Israelites waited centuries for the Messiah to appear. Generations came and went without the promise being fulfilled. Those who heard the prophecies from the lips of prophets would not see Christ during their lifetimes.

Would I have the faith to wait fourteen years, like Jacob, or an entire lifetime, like the Israelites, for a promise to be fulfilled?

Noboru doesn't have a promise or prophecy to hold on to—he can't be sure that Mikako will still want to be with him when she returns or if she'll return at all. Mikako, however, does have a spiritual experience to encourage her; on Agartha, an Earth-like planet, she sees a vision created by the Tarsians—an image of herself, a stronger and surer Mikako. It consoles her: "It will be all right. You will see him again."

In a world of immediate gratification, where answers to our problems are a Google search away and communication takes seconds rather than weeks (or light years), it's difficult to cultivate the patience God often asks of us. As with Mikako and Noboru, we are separated from God by space and time. But God is also intimately with us, always. We have a loving relationship with a holy being who remains faithful. Even as life, circumstances, and sin can seem to pull us further and further from God's embrace, the All Mighty is always there waiting for us.

It's in the doldrums of life that we can rely on God's character rather than fall into despair based on the circumstances around us. God has promised to save us from eternal death, forgive us as we fail, and guide us through the difficulties we encounter and pains we endure. We pray to be delivered from a toxic workplace, for the grace to forgive parents who have hurt us, or for relief from the chronic pain we're suffering. When an answer doesn't come immediately, we grow impatient and begin to lose faith. It's difficult to trust that God is still there and still cares. It's easy to forget the bigger picture and despair when resolutions take too much time or don't come at all.

In those moments, when the immediate and temporary are all we can see, our trust wavers. It feels like God isn't on the other end of our transmission or that we won't hear a reply for years. Or, perhaps, it takes years for us to understand and accept the reply. In those moments, I try to remember that God is eternal and enduring. No matter the situation, and no matter whether relief comes in this life or the next, the truth remains: God loves us. This message is repeated throughout Isaiah:

> "For the mountains may depart and the hills be removed, but my steadfast love shall not depart from you, and my covenant of peace shall not be removed, says the Lord, who has compassion on you."[2]

I find solace in the fact that God stands with me in every victory and every defeat. I depend on finding pockets of joy in this life and believe in the eternal celebration in the next. Just as the Israelites waited on God's promises, Jacob looked forward to his marriage with Rachel, and Mikako hoped to reunite with Noboru, I wait on God's word. I rely on God's promises, even during times that our relationship feels like it's long-distance.

As *Voices of a Distant Star* reaches its conclusion, both Noboru and Mikako recall the words of an earlier text. Mikako has been injured during the climactic battle, one in which most of her fleet is destroyed and her mecha partially dismembered. Noboru is now 24 years old and has just heard the news of that battle, which had happened eight years previously. But the comforting words they both recall speak through the despair, pain, and uncertainty: "I am here."

In all the noise of this life, when we feel that God is light years away, may we remember the same: God is here with us and is worth waiting for.

Key Scripture

"For in hope we were saved. Now hope that is seen is not hope. For who hopes for what is seen? But if we hope for what we do not see, we wait for it with patience." —Romans 8:24–25

Study Questions

1. What are you waiting on right now? Has it been a struggle to remain patient and faithful in the waiting?

2. What are some of the challenges of a long-distance relationship? How would you work through them? Do any of those challenges mirror the difficulties you have in communicating with God?

3. Do you sometimes feel that God is distant? How can you remind yourself that God is near and intimate during these times, no matter what your feelings tell you?

---

1. *Voices of a Distant Star*. Directed by Makoto Shinkai. ADV Films, 2002.
2. Isaiah 54:10.

27

A FLOWER IN THE SLUMS: JOY IN RUTH AND FINAL FANTASY VII

BY VICTORIA GRACE HOWELL

"Follow them. The yellow flowers."
—Aerith, *Final Fantasy VII Remake*[1]

Read: Ruth 1

Reflect: Aerith Gainsborough is the last of the Cetra, an ancient race with magical abilities. However, to most, she's simply a local florist who lives with her adopted mother in Sector Five.

Aerith grows up in a small room with no sunlight in a government laboratory. Every day, her birth mother is taken away to be experimented upon, and Aerith cries during her absence. She experiences crushing loneliness and fear on a regular basis. When she is around eight years old, she escapes the lab with her mother, but her mom doesn't survive for very long, dying on the streets in Aerith's arms. Thankfully, the little girl is found by a kindly woman who raises her in Sector Five, but Aerith still endures memories of her past traumas. She's also doggedly hunted by government agents who want to take her away to be a lab rat again.

Aerith has suffered so much, I'm surprised she's not bitter. Instead of resenting the scientists for killing her mother and hating the world for how unfair her life has been, Aerith is joyful. As a florist, she gives away her beautiful flowers with a smile, bringing happiness to others. Even as an abused child, she looks for beauty in life; later in the game, she returns to the laboratory and the player sees that, as a child, she drew a lovely mural of flowers and sunshine—painted buds growing on the gloom of a metal wall.

I admire (and sometimes envy) Aerith's joyfulness. I struggle with frustration when I encounter difficulties, such as the isolation brought on by COVID-19. It's tricky for me to look on the bright sides of situations and so much easier to let loneliness weigh on me. Sometimes I wonder why God lets me—and others—suffer. How are we supposed to keep our faith alive during tragedy and find joy even amid the darkest times in our lives?

I wonder if Ruth and Naomi ask these same questions after they lose their family in such a short span of time. They have to uproot their entire lives and move to escape a famine. In Ruth 1, it's revealed that Naomi takes the situation very hard, so much so that she changes her name from Naomi, which means "sweet," to Mara, which means "bitter."

Naomi reminds me of Cloud, the main character in *Final Fantasy VII*, who reacts to his trauma by isolating himself. Naomi tells her two daughters-in-law, Ruth and Orpah, to go back to their families because they have nothing to gain by staying with her. She is resigned to being alone.

Ruth, on the other hand, reminds me of Aerith. Though she grieves for her lost loved ones, she doesn't succumb to bitterness. Instead of returning to her family, as Orpah does, she sacrifices her needs to help Naomi:

> "Do not press me to leave you or to turn back from following you! Where you go, I will go; where you lodge, I will lodge; your people shall be my people, and your God my God. Where you die, I will die—there will I be buried. May the Lord do thus and so to me, and more as well, if even death parts me from you!"[2]

Ruth refuses to give up on her mother-in-law. Similarly, Aerith forms a bond with Cloud, helping him throughout the game as they travel through dangerous territory and fight mighty foes. She does this despite the danger of being discovered by Shinra.

Aerith's joy—an attitude that Cloud learns from, which helps him make peace with his own difficult life—is influenced by gratefulness and love. Aerith is thankful for her adopted mother, loves her new friends, and finds life in the world around her. She appreciates even the little things, like beautiful flowers. Aerith doesn't focus on the things she doesn't have, but on the things she does. Thankfulness like Aerith's can be a balm because it helps her make peace with circumstances that are beyond her control.

Notably, Aerith doesn't just tell Cloud to cheer up and look on the bright side of things. Neither does Ruth tell Naomi to change her name back because she's being ungrateful. Cloud isn't less of a hero than Aerith and Naomi isn't less faithful than Ruth because they struggled. Instead, the sad characters are given space to feel how they feel, to be human, to express their emotions. Aerith and Ruth stand by their companions, loving them as they are. And their joy, simply by existing, spreads.

Aerith's and Ruth's love is similar to the way God loves us. God wants to hear our praises, our pleas, and even our anger. Our Creator wants to comfort us. Sometimes, being joyful during suffering doesn't look like a smile; instead, it might look like steadfastness that things will be okay in the end, clutching onto a glimmer of hope, or simply waiting for the pain to heal.

Aerith's main theme in the *Crisis Core Final Fantasy VII* soundtrack is called "A Flower Blooming in the Slums." She manages to make flowers grow in unyielding soil where there is little greenery—and they are a representation of her own joy and the impact she has on others. Her favourite flowers are yellow lilies, which, appropriately, symbolize thankfulness and joy.

God doesn't give up on us when we struggle. Our Creator can make flowers grow even in the stubbornest soil. God inspires me to search for joy, to hunt through the darkness for light, even in the most difficult of times. Follow the yellow flowers and bloom.

Key Scripture

"Rejoice in hope, be patient in suffering, persevere in prayer." —Romans: 12:12

Study Questions

1. When you feel like Cloud and Naomi, sad, bitter, and hopeless, what do you think God's attitude towards you is?

2. When you are like Aerith and Ruth, thankful and brimming with joy, how can you best support others who are suffering?

3. What does joy look like when you're sad?

———————————————

1. *Final Fantasy VII Remake*. PlayStation 4, Square Enix, 2020.
2. Ruth 1:16–17.

28

REFLECTIONS OF IDENTITY IN 2001: A SPACE ODYSSEY

BY NATHAN CAMPBELL

"I am putting myself to the fullest possible use, which is all, I think, that any conscious entity can ever hope to do."
  —HAL 9000, *2001: A Space Odyssey* [1]

Read: 1 Corinthians 13

Reflect: In 1964, when Stanley Kubrick and Arthur C. Clarke set out to make a good science fiction movie, humankind was taking its first steps into the ocean of space beyond the shores of planet Earth. Just a few years prior, in 1961, Yuri Gagarin became the first human to travel into space. Kubrick's goal was to tell a story about "[humankind's] relationship to the universe."[2] The effort culminated in the classic film *2001: A Space Odyssey*, released in 1968, eight months before the fantastic voyage of Apollo 8's Christmas Eve circumnavigation of the moon, and nearly a year before Neil Armstrong's lunar footprints.

The film follows Dr. David Bowman and Dr. Frank Poole on a mission to Jupiter after the discovery of an alien monolith on the Moon. The monolith sent a radio signal to Jupiter, and the humans have been sent to investigate. Their spacecraft, *Discovery One*, is mainly controlled by HAL, an artificial intelligence who tries to murder the astronauts on the journey. Bowman alone survives the trip, deactivates HAL, and makes it to Jupiter to discover another monolith orbiting the planet. Upon further investigation, Bowman is pulled into a vortex of light and has visions of himself as he grows old. In the end, he transforms into a fetus-like "Star-Child" who is suspended in light and hovers in space beside Earth.

Most science fiction film and television productions prior to the release of *2001: A Space Odyssey*, with a few exceptions, deal with the standard pulp fare of dastardly robots or bug-eyed aliens threatening worlds. Clarke and Kubrick deviated from the zeitgeist of this period by probing into the existential. Famously, the film deliberately leaves the questions it raises unanswered. Clarke himself even states: "If anyone understands it on the first viewing, we've failed in our intention."[3]

As a work of art, the movie cannot be reduced to a single interpretation. We can, however, like the characters in the film, peer into the surface of the monolith and perhaps see "in a mirror, dimly" some reflection of our own deeper needs. The film encourages us to consider the role that the monolith plays in regards to human growth, identity, and our need to know our value in the universe.

Two questions at the core of a Christian's place and value in the universe are 1) Who is God? and 2) Who am I?

Without a clear understanding of the answer to one, an answer to the other is lacking. Understanding ourselves and our relationship to God is more than mere self-awareness. We want to be known, not simply by collecting numerous acquaintances but by having our true selves be fully understood, appreciated, and loved. Theologian N.T. Wright states, "Love is the deepest mode of knowing, because it is in love that, while completely engaging with reality other than itself, affirms and celebrates that other-than-self reality."[4] We want the answer to "Who am I?" to be reflected completely and honestly via others as well as through ourselves.

2001: A Space Odyssey's monolith could represent God reaching out to humankind to speak to and shape our identity. Each time a character responds in kind by seeking answers from the monolith, change occurs. Looking to find a reflection in the stark, empty slab, each interaction with the monolith drives the characters towards a more perfected humanity. From the very first scene of the movie, which shows a pre-human ape kick-starting his evolutionary development, to to the final scene, which depicts a dying Bowman reaching towards the monolith and transforming into the Star-Child, the characters find the next iteration of their identity—a deepening and changing understanding of their final destiny.

While the monolith of the film helps to enlighten those who come into contact with it, the mechanisms and designs behind this change are left to mystery. Thankfully, neither our divine connection to God nor our Creator's purposeful love for us is as shrouded. In Christ, we may find some of these answers to our questions. However, Christ, as he often does, turns the questions on their head.

Rather than answering "Who is God?", Jesus reflects the questions back to us: "who do *you* say that I am?"[5] He also says what matters about our identity is not who we or others say we are; it is who *he* says we are.[6]

We are those who are infinitely loved. Thus, the answer comes back to the focus of 1 Corinthians 13: love. As Paul writes, if we do not have love, we ultimately have nothing and can therefore give nothing. Truth without love is noise. Charity without love feeds a body but starves a soul. Because we are loved, we can love and affirm others.

Real love shapes our identity in ways we don't always comprehend, allowing us to become fully ourselves while losing ourselves to another. N.T. Wright writes:

> "The lover affirms the reality and otherness of the beloved. Love does not seek to collapse the beloved into terms of itself; and even though it may speak of losing itself in the beloved, such a loss always turns out to be a true finding. In the familiar paradox, one becomes fully oneself when losing oneself to another. In the fact of love, in short, both parties are simultaneously affirmed."[7]

Christ died for us not because we earned his sacrifice, but because he is love, and he loves infinitely. In this love, we can find our own monolith experience; a transformative connection with the divine. Christ transforms us into new creations. Once we have a firm grasp on who God says we are—that we are God's beloved—we can then find our truest identity, and we are finally and fully known.

Key Scripture

> "So if anyone is in Christ, there is a new creation: everything old has passed away; see, everything has become new!" —2 Corinthians 5:17–21

Study Questions

1. In what do you most often find your identity?

2. How does knowing what Jesus thinks of you change how you perceive yourself?

3. How can knowing what Jesus thinks of your identity change how you interact with and love others who are still searching to find their own true identity?

---

1. *2001: A Space Odyssey.* Directed by Stanley Kubrick. Metro-Goldwyn-Mayer, 1968.
2. Clarke, Arthur C. *The Lost Worlds of 2001.* New American Library, 1972.
3. McAleer, Neil. *Arthur C. Clarke: The Authorized Biography.* Contemporary Books, 1993.
4. Wright, N.T. *Surprised by Scripture: Engaging Contemporary Issues.* New York: HarperOne, 2014.
5. Luke 9:20.
6. Matthew 7:23.
7. Wright, N.T. *The New Testament and the People of God: Christian Origins and the Question of God.* Augsburg Fortress, 1992.

29

THE VALUE OF CYBORGS AND SECOND-CLASS CITIZENS

BY ALLISON ALEXANDER

"I am not human. I am a cyborg. I am a mechanic. That's all I am... right?"
—Cinder, *Cinder* by Marissa Meyer[1]

Read: Psalm 73

Reflect: Cinder is a cyborg. Because she was in a fire as a child, her left hand and leg are made of metal, her vertebrae and the tissue around her heart are synthetic, and her eyes are human-made. In the world of Marissa Meyer's Lunar Chronicles, this means she is a second-class citizen without basic human rights. She's considered the "property" of her stepmother, who uses her for slave labour and looks down on her as less than human. Her stepmother even uses Cinder's lack of tear ducts to dehumanize her, taunting Cinder with the fact that the cyborg can't cry. She also sends Cinder to be a "volunteer" test subject as part of the kingdom's ongoing experiments to cure a plague.

Cinder is a talented mechanic, a kind-hearted person with a dry sense of humour, a friend, a beloved sister, and a down-to-earth influence on the story's prince. But in her mind, all that fades away when confronted by society's prejudice. She devalues herself because that is what her culture has taught her to do. She is worthless. She is nothing. She is cyborg.

Cinder's fight to live, to be valued by others, and to value herself strikes home for me, as someone with a disability. The Western world often sees people with illnesses and disabilities as "less than," because we can't do everything that healthy people can, because we aren't "contributing" to society, because we are a drain on resources and a burden to others (even those who care about us), and because our bodies are different than theirs.

I empathize with Asaph, the writer of Psalm 73 (likely the same Asaph who is mentioned in 1 Chronicles 6:39, a prophet and songwriter from King David's court), who is jealous of the privileged people around him:

> "For they have no pain; their bodies are sound and sleek. They are not in trouble as others are; they are not plagued like other people."[2]

This Psalm is written from the perspective of a suffering person. When you're in pain, it seems like no one else understands, like no one else is hurting as much as you are. In reality, everyone has their own pain. But that doesn't mean yours is invalid. And there are many, many prejudices that exist in our world working to invalidate others' experiences and punish minorities for simply existing. These are the people that Asaph calls "wicked," people who oppress others, who speak hurtful words, who are full of pride, who profit from their prejudice—"always at ease, they increase in riches."[3]

Though Cinder fights for her life throughout the story and, at first, just wants to escape and survive, she internalizes some of society's negative views. When she meets Prince Kai, she is immediately attracted by his kindness. When they continue to encounter each other and become friends, she tries to keep him at a distance despite the romantic feelings growing between them. He doesn't know she is a cyborg, and she is afraid he will reject her if he finds out the truth. Her fears are confirmed when he sees an x-ray of her body, with all her human-made parts on display, and looks at it with disgust. He doesn't know it's an x-ray of *her* body, but it's enough for Cinder to believe he could never love her as she is.

And yet the kindness he shows to her, when she's a "nobody" and he's a prince, has an impact on her:

> "She raised her eyebrows in a look that she hoped conveyed how much she was all right with him leaving her. After all, he was a prince. The most powerful men and women on Earth had summoned him. She understood. And yet he was still here, with her."

This paragraph about Kai reminds me of Jesus' attitude. He could have spent his time on Earth with kings. Instead, he spent it with the least of us. He still does. He values the broken, the sick, the hungry, the weak. The Jews. The Greeks. The cyborgs.

I get frustrated when people, especially Christians, don't accept others as Jesus does—when they say that you aren't valuable until you're healed, until you lose weight, until you stop being gay, until you agree with a specific doctrine. Yes, Jesus loves everyone and so do I, they say, but you aren't truly being faithful unless you fit this precise mould of what *I* think it means to be a believer. Yes, Jesus loves everyone and so do I, they say, but if your skin is a certain colour, I'm still going to be suspicious of you until you prove yourself trustworthy. These prejudices are falsehoods drilled into us by our dominant cultural assumptions about being human.

I get frustrated with myself when similar thoughts creep up on me—when I treat someone else as less than. I'm not exempt from being prejudiced and making cultural assumptions. Even though I've suffered for being a part of a minority, I turn around and cause others to suffer, too. Like Asaph, I've been stupid and ignorant:

> "When my soul was embittered,
> When I was pricked in heart,
> I was stupid and ignorant:
> I was like a brute beats
>   toward you.
> Nevertheless I am continually
>   with you;
> You hold my right hand.
> You guide me with your counsel,
> And afterward you will receive
>   me with honor."[4]

In the Lunar Chronicles, Kai confronts his own prejudice and fights for justice. As the leader of a country, he can make real change happen, and he does. Cinder herself discovers she is prejudiced against a different group of people, the Lunars, and must confront those attitudes within herself. Her story is about understanding that appearance isn't what makes a person good or evil, that lies are often spread across society to benefit the privileged and the wealthy, and that morality isn't black and white, even though we'd like it to be.

Psalm 73 begins with, "Truly God is good to the upright, to those who are pure in heart,"[5] a statement that assumes the experience of God's goodness somehow depends on whether one is righteous. Part of Asaph's journey, and his admittance of ignorance, is moving away from that statement. The Psalm ends with "But for me it is good to be near God."[6] Asaph's understanding of goodness is transformed in the presence of God in a way that doesn't depend on perfection, meritocracy, privilege, or anything else. He moves from a performance-oriented goodness to a grace-oriented goodness.

Our own understanding of God's grace starts with the knowledge that God loves us, no matter who we are, no matter what we look like, no matter where we come from. Our bodies may fail, but God is our strength forever. Jew or Greek, slave or free, cyborg or Lunar, we are all one in Christ.

Key Scripture

> "There is no longer Jew or Greek, there is no longer slave or free, there is no longer male and female; for all of you are one in Christ Jesus."
> —Galatians 3:28

Study Questions

> 1. In what ways do you de-value yourself? What are some ways you can work towards valuing yourself and knowing you are loved by God?

> 2. Have you ever been discriminated against? What did it feel like? Have you ever discriminated against someone else? What did *that* feel like?

> 3. Why do you think Christians like rules? What happens when the rules are replaced with love?

---

1. Meyer, Marissa. *Cinder.* Fewer & Friends, 2012.
2. Psalm 73:4–5.
3. Psalm 73:12.
4. Psalm 73:21–24.
5. Psalm 73:1.
6. Psalm 73:28.

30

WAR, PEACE, AND WONDERBEASTS

BY KYLE RUDGE

"You can't end a war by fighting it."
—Kipo, *Kipo and the Age of Wonderbeasts*[1]

Read: Luke 22:14–23; 47–53

Reflect: *Kipo and the Age of Wonderbeasts*, an animated TV series adapted from a webcomic, takes place in a post-apocalyptic world where an unspoken disaster has sent all humans underground. Evolved animals, known as mutants or "mutes," live in Last Vistas—the world above the burrows. Domestic cats have evolved into intelligent lumberjacks who love pancakes (somehow, this makes perfect sense). Timbercats live among the trees and practice a form of ancestral worship in which they honour past warriors. Wolves manufacture simple machines and use technology to advance their own agendas. Each faction has their own idea of what the world should be, what happiness is, and how power is attained.

After a mutant attack on the burrow of our plucky

hero, Kipo, she is separated from her collective and her father. She is forced into the world above the burrow and encounters the various warring factions. Her kindness surprises every mute she meets, and she leaves an impression on each of the tribes she visits.

Throughout the show's three seasons, war continues to boil, and Kipo tries everything to be reunited with her father. Along the way, she makes friends and becomes determined to end the conflict between the animal tribes.

In the third season, Kipo has the opportunity to strike back against her greatest enemy with extreme force, but she refrains from doing so. She insists that violent actions demand violent reactions and refuses to be part of that cycle. She says:

> "This fighting going on between mutants and humans has been happening for centuries. And I could win today's battle, but some other humans would come along to continue the war. That's because you can't end a war by fighting it."

This phrase strikes deep into the heart of so many of my personal struggles. When someone betrays me (or even cuts me off in traffic), I demand justice. But, if I am truly honest, what I really want is vengeance, power, and control. As I get older, I grow more and more convinced none of those things are actually worth it.

When I read the biblical account of Jesus, especially his peaceful behaviour in the four gospels, I am struck by how often human nature betrays us. Our primal instinct is to retaliate, to hit back harder than we were hit, to win, and to dominate. Yet, that is not the way Jesus intends for us to live.

Luke 22 describes Judas's betrayal, the Passover, and the iconic Last Supper. Jesus shares his final meal with his friends who have followed him devoutly for all this time. They don't know it is the final meal, but Jesus knows. He starts a new ritual, which we now know as communion, breaking a loaf of bread and pouring out wine to be shared among everyone. "Do this in remembrance of me," he says.[2]

The disciples are probably confused, but they are willing to trust that Jesus' prophetic statements will make sense later, when it is time for them to understand. But then Jesus says something specific and startling: "the one who betrays me is with me, and his hand is on this table."[3]

The disciples immediately start trying to figure out who Jesus is talking about. I can imagine the suspicions, accusations, and defensive rebuttals running rampant. But Jesus doesn't seem concerned with naming his betrayer.

Jesus retreats to the Mount of Olives to pray, and he pours out his heart to God, asking for relief and the strength to endure. When he returns to the disciples, who have long since fallen asleep, he notices one is missing. Then, Judas shows up with an angry crowd and seals Jesus' fate with a kiss. The disciples take up arms in response. If ever there were a time to fight, it's now. One of the disciples swings his sword and slices off the ear of one of the slaves present.

If this were a movie, the epic fight scene would go here. Instead, Jesus heals the wounded man.

Jesus knows he does not win this war by fighting. Though his followers are expecting a great military leader who will overthrow the government for their freedom, that is not who Jesus is.

The next chapter of Luke details Jesus' crucifixion and death. He dies on the very cross he's forced to carry through the streets, on a back that has been whipped raw and bloody.

If Jesus had chosen to retaliate, to smite down his crucifiers, he would have perpetuated the cycle of retaliatory violence. Instead, by dying, he puts an end to the assumptions that violence and power are necessary.

Like Christ, Kipo acts peacefully when she could retaliate. She tells her friends, her army, to stand down, even though they have a prime opportunity to end the current conflict and get vengeance. Kipo knows that it would only be a matter of time before the war continued and more lives were lost. She faces her friends, humans and mutants of all types, each of them longing for retribution, and implores them to choose the harder path: peace over vengeance:

"So I am asking you, my people, my friends, to choose to stop fighting and break the cycle."

While our lives might not be as dramatic as a post-apocalyptic war between humans and mutants, we have opportunities to fight or stand back almost every day. The driver who cut me off was wrong, but if I retaliate by speeding up and cutting *them* off, it only perpetuates dangerous driving. If I yell at my children, I teach them to do the same to others. If I wear my anger on my sleeve, I may win the battle, but I won't find peace on the other side, and the war, sadly, continues.

There is a difference between being passive and choosing pacifism. Ending the cycle of war does not mean you become a doormat for your enemies to tread upon. It doesn't mean seeing abuse and walking on by. Instead, we are called to creativity in finding peaceful solutions to conflict. That could mean giving the driver who cut me off the benefit of the doubt—maybe they just received the worst news of their life and made a mistake in their emotional state. That could mean showing compassion instead of anger to shut down an argument. That could mean removing yourself from a violent situation to ensure your own safety. Or that could mean, like Kipo, you organize an elaborate theme party and invite your enemies as the guests of honour.

Both Jesus and Kipo wanted to change the order of things from a system of violence to a system of peace. In addition to seeking creative ways to resolve conflict, we can also look for positive ways to counter the violence of racism, classism, and other repressive movements. We make friends with the marginalized and with our enemies. We advocate for just laws. We heal instead of hurt. These actions don't come automatically and we often have to work at changing our way of thinking.

We can follow Jesus' example and break the cycle. We can't end a war by fighting it.

Key Scripture

"Blessed are the peacemakers, for they will be called children of God." —Matthew 5:9

Study Questions

1. What wars do you fight that never seem to end?

2. Kindness in the face of violence often comes at a cost. What do you think that cost is, and how can you prepare yourself to pay it?

3. What would your family, friends, and workplace look like if peace prevailed instead of a desire to get even?

---

1. *Kipo and the Age of Wonderbeasts.* "Requiem for a Dave," season 3, episode 7. Directed by Bridget Underwood. NBCUniversal, 2020.
2. Luke 22:19.
3. Luke 22:21.

31

CAST OUT THE SHADOWS: BAPTISM AND SHE-RA

BY ASHLEY MOWERS

Catra: "Adora... you should have stayed away. Why did you come back? We both know I don't matter..."
Adora: "You matter to me."
    —*She-Ra and the Princesses of Power*[1]

Read: 1 John 4

Reflect: Religion made me anxious for most of my childhood and a significant portion of my young adult life. Some of this apprehension was enhanced by poor, however well-intentioned, children's ministry. (I challenge you to answer the five-year-old who asks, "What if someone *dies* during their baptism?" Nine a.m. is too early for such conversations.) As I grew older, my anxiety became entangled in unspoken social concerns: What if I turn into someone I don't like? What if I choose the wrong denomination? What if I learn something new and they kick me out? What if... what if... what if... My head was heavy with anxiety and I had the posture to show for it.

I think this is why I gravitate toward Catra from the TV show *She-Ra and the Princesses of Power*. Catra grows up with Adora (a.k.a. She-Ra) in the Evil Horde, and they are best friends at the start of the show. When Adora realizes the Horde is oppressive and leaves to become She-Ra, Catra is angry and blames Adora for abandoning her.

Initially, Catra appears self-assured, shrewd, determined, and sometimes too-clever-by-half. Yet, not too far into the series, we learn about her fear of abandonment. Despite her shrewd and ambitious performance, what ultimately holds Catra back is her initial inability to overcome shame and accept forgiveness. In the third episode of the final season, this unhealthy cycle motivates her to act desperately: while she successfully saves Glimmer, one of the main characters, Catra needlessly sacrifices herself to Horde Prime, the antagonist.

Horde Prime is an uncomfortably well-written villain. While he acknowledges the strong bonds between Adora and her friends—and especially with Catra—he offers a hollow performance of that loving, communal spirit. His use of empty platitudes and syrupy intimacies throughout Episode Three of Season Five are calculating and unscrupulous:

> "You are beloved in my sight, and this is how you repay me?"
> "All beings must suffer to become pure."
> "Behold the purest among you, one to be honored."
> "Cast out the shadows. Cast out the shadows. Cast out—"

Some of this may sound vaguely familiar. Writer Noelle Stevenson intentionally based Horde Prime on cult leaders and their use of coercion to feed their own egos, and this parasitic nature is illustrated perfectly. While God desires a covenantal relationship with each of us, and baptism reflects a decision to enter into such a relationship, Prime *needs* the populations of entire planets to sustain his illusion of immortality and impotence. He utilizes a similar ritual to subjugate his followers. His horde is not "fearfully and wonderfully made"—they are enslaved.

To add to the horror, Stevenson and her team designed his ship on contemporary and megachurch architecture. Because she's a master at her craft, the effect is an upsetting and necessarily harsh depiction of indoctrination. So when Catra chooses self-destruction to escape her shame, I felt grief on three levels: one, watching the traumatic fate of a beloved character; two, witnessing a ritual I recognize as beautiful and restorative being used to enforce uniformity and coercion; and three, knowing this kind of manipulation has and continues to occur in some congregations.

What comforts me is that this isn't what the rite of baptism and the Christian community is *meant* to be. Where Prime subjugates, Christ emboldens. Where his clones are brainwashed, Christ's disciples are forgiven and welcomed. Prime may refer to his clones as his "flock," but he does little to shepherd them from harm.

The following is an Orthodox blessing of the baptismal water, which reflects nothing of Prime's murky, cultic ritual:

"All creation magnifies you, who have manifested yourself among us. You hallowed the streams of Jordan, sending down upon them from heaven your Holy Spirit, and you crushed the heads of the dragons who lurked there.

"Wherefore, O King who loves humanity, come now and sanctify this water, by the indwelling of your Holy Spirit."[2]

Prime doesn't demonstrate true love for the Etherians, and there's nothing sacred in his slime. The Princesses of Power, however, are an example of what the Church is meant to be. The Princesses are an alliance of magical women who fight against the oppressive Horde, strive to help others, and support each other. Their goal is the complete opposite of Prime's, because they invite others into true community.

My favourite part of a baptismal service is when the newly baptized is welcomed by their church. Sometimes this is demonstrated by polite clapping and well-concealed tears. The one I most recently attended was celebrated with audible cheering and whooping. Baptism isn't just for the candidate; it's for the congregation, too. It's a ceremony that reminds us what the church is and what we're all meant to become together. It's a sacrament demonstrating what it means to dedicate oneself to others. Being baptized is an accepted invitation into a sacred story: the story of God's love for us and our love for each other, like 1 John 4 relates.

1 John was written to believers and contains a lot of black and white imagery: light vs. darkness, Christ vs. antichrists, love of the world vs. God, sin vs. righteousness.

It's also very much focused on love. The community we are baptized into loves one another, for God is love, and God lives in us.

This kind of loving invitation and celebration is what She-Ra and the Princesses of Power offer Catra (and Entrapta! And even Hordak!). It's not always easy—Catra struggles with post-traumatic stress from her experiences. She lashes out and is rooted in her self-hatred. But the princesses' demonstration of kind, patient love allows her the opportunity to heal, reconcile, and uniquely aid the team.

It can be difficult to believe this kind of community exists. Perhaps you're still recovering from a tough religious upbringing or an upsetting church experience. Maybe you've never been baptized, or never thought much about it if you have. Whatever it is, it's important to recognize that your story isn't finished yet, and you don't have to experience it alone. I've experienced my fair share of Hordak Primes and have felt like I'd never shake free from their grasp. But when the Church is rejecting evil and imitating God's love, there will be people there to catch you. And when the Church reflects Christ's light, it can truly cast out the shadows.

Key Scripture

"Let all that you do be done in love."
—1 Corinthians 16:14

Study Questions

1. Read the liturgy of baptism in your own tradition or a tradition you are familiar with. What promises are made? How is your current faith community upholding those promises?

2. Identify other groups and communities you are a part of. How do you reflect Jesus within you while you are present with those groups? If you don't feel you do, reflect on what may be keeping you from doing so.

3. When was the last time you felt "fearfully and wonderfully made"? What efforts do you make to remind others of this in their own lives?

---

1. *She-Ra and the Princesses of Power.* "Save the Cat," season 5, episode 5. Directed by Roy Burdine and Jen Bennett. Netflix, 2020.
2. Huck, Gabe. *A Triduum Sourcebook.* Liturgy Training Pubns, 1983.

32

HEROES AND MISFITS: THE IMPORTANCE OF FAILURE IN OVERWATCH AND THE BIBLE

BY DAN BERGMAN

"You know, the world could always use more heroes."
—Tracer, *Overwatch*[1]

Read: 1 Corinthians 1:18–31

Reflect: At the end of the 21st century, the world finds itself in peril again. The mysterious terrorist organization Talon threatens to initiate a war that will consume the world. Their belief is that humanity is strengthened through conflict: "Those who fall will be forgotten... those who rise up will be remembered forever."

At the same time, another war has begun, due to mounting tensions between humans and the artificially intelligent robots known as Omnics. There are those who believe that Omnics deserve the same rights and privileges afforded to humans; others believe it is only a matter of time before they wipe out humankind. Around the world, gangs and evil corporations are rising up to take advantage of the disarray.

But! The heroic strike force that successfully led the world into an era of peace, stability, and scientific advancement 30 years ago has been recalled. Wrongfully disbanded and criminalized by the United Nations years ago, the members of this organization who weren't presumed dead became independent scientists, mercenaries, or rogues. Thanks to the call from their defacto leader, Winston, the group successfully saved Paris from an Omnic attack and are at work to bring peace once again. Overwatch is back!

We've just scratched the surface of the story of the team-based first person shooter, *Overwatch*. But you'd never know the story from simply playing the game.

Overwatch is a player-versus-player objective game in which you are immediately thrown into the action. There are (pretty much) no story missions, no campaigns, no side quests. Instead, the developers chose to flesh out the story through supplemental media. Animated shorts, comics, short stories, in-game easter eggs, and character conversations all give insight to the *Overwatch* timeline of events and character backstories.

At the time of writing, there are currently 32 playable heroes, some who side with Overwatch and others who side with Talon or other nefarious groups. *Overwatch 2* is set to release soon, and its focus will be story missions—so who knows how much more of the plot will be uncovered! But I digress...

"What a bunch of misfits and freaks we got here—I *love it!*"

This is one of my favourite lines from *Overwatch*,

spoken by the half-insane demolition enthusiast, Junkrat, while you're with your team waiting for the game to start.

Without any of the background information on these characters, you might assume they are all cookie-cutter heroes—noble and flawless. But after learning more about them, I have to agree with Junkrat.

Winston, a genetically enhanced, super-intelligent gorilla, was left orphaned by the scientists who raised him —and yet, he ended up being the one to recall the Overwatch team. Tracer, a time-jumping adventurer, piloted an experimental aircraft that failed and caused her to experience "chronal disassociation" (an inability to control her place in time and space)—but this led to her developing a unique set of time-jumping abilities. Genji, a cyborg ninja, lived a tormented life before joining Overwatch because his brother mortally wounded him—but he became strong when he found peace with his new body and forgave his brother. Baptiste, an elite combat medic, carried out missions for Talon that resulted in civilian casualties—but once he realized his wrongdoing, he fled to pursue humanitarian work. Mina Liao, an expert in artificial intelligence, helped design the Omnics with good intentions and was wracked with guilt before she died— but her crowning achievement, Echo, carries Mina's personality in her advanced AI, continuing the good work she began.

In spite of—and in some cases, *because* of—these individuals' failures, sins, and plain bad luck, they became heroes, choosing to use their talents to make the world a better place.

These characters' stories are believable because no one is one-dimensionally good. We all have hardships to overcome, and we don't always make the right decisions even when we have good intentions.

You can find many "misfits and freaks" in the Bible. God partners with all kinds of people in the Old Testament and the New, and every one of them has their own story of failure woven in with their success.

Moses, the bringer of the Ten Commandments, delivers the Israelites from slavery in Egypt (even though he is full of excuses as to why he shouldn't be the one for the task). Eve, the first woman, gives into Satan's temptation, yet she becomes the mother of humanity. Jonah, a prophet, finds several ways to cowardly avoid God's call to save the people of Nineveh before repenting. Naomi, Ruth's stepmother, is bitter towards God due to the death of her husband and sons, and she is crucial to Ruth's journey in finding her place in the world and becoming part of Christ's lineage. Peter, one of Jesus' disciples, denies Jesus at the time of his crucifixion, but later becomes the "rock" of the church, building it up in spite of intense persecution. Rachel, a shepherd, is manipulative (for example, demanding that her husband, Jacob, have a child with her maid, and stealing her father's household gods), yet she plays a crucial role in the Genesis story. Paul, the apostle, kills Christians as heretics before repenting and authoring much of the New Testament.

It was, at first, shocking to realize that all these biblical heroes were failures. Why is it that God would use such broken people? Where were all the perfect people who could flawlessly execute God's plan?

I was brought up in the Christian church, and "perfection" was something that I used to have a hard time dealing with. As a young Christ-follower, it was hard to read the Bible and *not* see it as a list of dos-and-don'ts. Whenever I failed to measure up to the standard set out by Scripture, even in the smallest of ways, I thought about what might await me in eternity as a consequence of those actions, and I would be filled with guilt and fear.

As I matured in my faith, however, I continued to learn about the person of Jesus. He didn't spend his time on Earth condemning those the world saw as sinful. Instead, Jesus spent his time with them, comforting them, forgiving them. Paul says in Romans 8 that there is no condemnation for those who are in Jesus, but that he sets us free from the law of sin and death if we follow him.

The truth is, nobody is perfect but God alone. We can see this from Scripture, and we can see it in our own lives. Our *hope* is found in how God works in spite of our failures, sins, and plain bad luck. In our weaknesses, we see God's strength and perfection even more clearly. In our failures, we see the person of Jesus, who has wiped our slate clean and redeemed us. What great news!

When I'm feeling like a misfit, freak, or failure, I'm encouraged by the stories of heroism found in the characters of *Overwatch*, and by the stories of God's people found in Scripture. Much more importantly, I'm encouraged by the fact that Christ is enough for me, and that God loves me for who I am.

Key Scripture

"...but he said to me, 'My grace is sufficient for you, for power is made perfect in weakness.' So, I will boast all the more gladly of my weaknesses, so that

the power of Christ may dwell in me. Therefore I am content with weaknesses, insults, hardships, persecutions, and calamities for the sake of Christ; for whenever I am weak, then I am strong."
—2 Corinthians 12:9–10

Study Questions

1. What are some ways that you have felt like a failure? Do those shortcomings make you feel guilty?

2. Who else can you think of (real or fictional) that has achieved some kind of success through their failures?

3. What's a step you can take towards accepting that God does not expect nor require perfection from you?

---

1.   *Overwatch*. Microsoft Windows, Blizzard Entertainment, 2016.

33

DOING GOOD IN AN UPSIDE-DOWN WORLD

BY MATT CIVICO

"Do you ever feel cursed?"
　　—Jim Hopper, *Stranger Things*[1]

Read: Romans 7 and 8

Reflect: Jim Hopper is a pop culture hero now, but this wasn't always the case. When Will Byers goes missing in Season One of *Stranger Things*, Police Chief Hopper is a hurting man; most people would keep their children away from him. He's no hero, but he's all Hawkins has.

Hopper is no stranger to the conflict in Romans 7:14–25, in which the Apostle Paul discusses acting sinfully despite good intentions. Sometimes, we are stopped from doing the right thing because of external forces, like evil government agents or the Upside Down, but often our struggles come from the inside. Hopper's self-loathing, depicted in his substance abuse and negligence, recalls Paul's own cry: "Wretched man that I am!"[2]

After the death of his daughter and the end of his

marriage, Hopper doesn't know what to do with himself. His hope for a good return on his life and service is crushed, but the chief doesn't want to give up on life. He still loves fiercely, yet his undirected love, his passion, is as likely to do harm as it is to help. He needs to reorient his love to the world around him to use it for good.

North African bishop Augustine had a novel idea about evil: it is nothing. It's literally not a thing. Evil is the absence of goodness. Evil exists in the space left by less good versions of ultimately *good* things. This means evil and sin aren't in direct competition with goodness, rather they're parasites living off the life of goodness. Evil can be described as the inversion of the good, or goodness turned upside-down.

Because of the trauma he's experienced, his frustration, and his unwillingness to be vulnerable, Hopper's goodness has been turned upside-down. He feels cursed, like his life is out of his control, and he's not wrong.

We all exist under the "curse" of sin, which wars with our desire to do right. The Bible tells a series of stories about how humans mess up and how God redeems mistakes. Finally, God comes to us as a human being. Jesus, through his life, death, and resurrection, breaks the cycle of death, which we alone are not strong enough to break.

All creation—every fish, flower, and tree frog—"waits with eager longing"[3] for the time when all things "will be set free from bondage to decay and will obtain the freedom of the glory of the children of God."[4] Where is the cure? How can creation be set free? I wish it was as easy as "accept Jesus as your lord and saviour and you'll be sin-free." But Paul tells us that all of creation groans while we wait for redemption.

We all groan inwardly from the weight of sin. Christ has set us free, but we still feel, experience, commit, and see sin all around us. What are we to do while we wait in the lingering darkness for the promise of indestructible life? Jim Hopper provides an unlikely example of how love fuels good work in an upside-down world of sin and brokenness.

Season One of *Stranger Things* reveals that Hopper lost a daughter to cancer. Her death was the catalyst for his grief, depression, and subsequent terrible decision-making. But it's also what motivates him to help Joyce find her son. He knows what the loss of a child feels like, and doesn't want her to experience what he has already gone through.

It takes the hope of redemption, however fragile, to reorient Hopper's love to the world around him. He could not save his daughter, but he will save Will Byers (and later, Hawkins itself) even if it costs him everything. Living a life of love and choosing to do good isn't easy when evils great and small lie close at hand. The risks of standing up to that evil are huge.

Hopper's transformation isn't easy, and it involves pain (in his case, emotional *and* physical). Service often looks like suffering, and it's tempting to avoid it so we don't feel that discomfort.

However, Hopper demonstrates that how we serve points to what we love. According to Augustine, people are not fundamentally what they believe, think, or even do —we are what we love. Timothy Keller writes something similar in *Making Sense of God*:

> "What we call human virtues are nothing more than forms of love... courage is loving your neighbour's well-being more than your own safety."[5]

With this definition of goodness, Hopper's slow awakening from burn-out cop to small-town champion begins to make sense. "You know what I would give for another chance," he tells Joyce, Will's mother. The chief, broken by sin and still sinning, groans for redemption. And so, he serves, and he does good in service of hope he cannot see but cannot stop desiring.

Hopper's story shows that loving service doesn't have to be perfect, and it certainly doesn't lead to perfection. In Seasons Two and Three of *Stranger Things*, he struggles with control and impatience, which can be considered lesser loves. However, when faced with suffering he can't ignore, suffering he understands thanks to his acquaintance with brokenness, he is able to love and serve. He is empowered by the hope that love might one day end suffering. He commits to this service even when the objects of his love do not always return his feelings in the ways he'd like. Eleven willfully rebels against his vices, and Joyce is unwilling, or unable, to return his love.

But Hopper's love isn't conditional on whether others love him back. He loves on with the kind of hope that Paul writes about in Romans: "For in hope we were saved. Now hope that is seen is not hope. For who hopes for what is seen? But if we hope for what we do not see, we wait for it with patience."[6]

Our labouring for love in a fallen world is prefigured by Christ's own suffering service. As surely as Jesus was lifted up on a cross to suffer on our behalf, we will be raised up in resurrection glory. By God's grace, we will taste this new life in the world, and our own labours of love will point a groaning creation to the One who will swallow up death in victory.

Key Scripture

> "For through the law I died to the law, so that I might live to God. I have been crucified with Christ; and it is no longer I who live, but it is Christ who lives in me. And the life I now live in the flesh I live by faith in the Son of God, who loved me and gave himself for me."
> —Galatians 2:19–20

Study Questions

1. How does your perspective on suffering impact how you view God's love?

2. Why does it matter that we, like Hopper, try to do good, even though we fail?

3. Think of your most common struggles. How might Augustine's concept of "rightly ordered loves" help you think more clearly about the desires at the root of those struggles?

---

1. *Stranger Things.* "The Weirdo on Maple Street," season 1, episode 2. Directed by The Duffer Brothers. Netflix, 2016.

2. Romans 7:24.
3. Romans 8:19.
4. Romans 8:20.
5. Keller, Timothy. *Making Sense of God: An Invitation to the Skeptical.* Viking, 2016.
6. Romans 8:24–25.

34

I SEE UNDEAD PEOPLE: THREE SPIRITUAL LESSONS FROM ZOMBIE APOCALYPSE FILMS

BY ELLEN ELLIOTT

"You just can't trust anyone. The first girl I let into my life and she tries to eat me."

—Columbus, *Zombieland*[1]

Read: Psalm 27

Reflect: I have to admit, I detest zombies. I dislike sewer rats, slow drivers, and math, too—but mostly zombies. It's not the gore I mind so much as the terrifying thought of an unreasonable, lumbering, undead menace, slowly coming to devour my brain. And there's nothing I can do about it. Zombies never stop coming after you. EVER.

Yet, I seem to be in the minority. Ever since the first zombie movie, *White Zombie*, premiered in 1932, the genre has increased in popularity and scope. Now there are Nazi zombies, airborne zombies, and even zombie romances. And while each zombie movie is unique, they follow similar rules. For instance, most successful zombie movies focus on ordinary people trying their best to survive. Also, with few exceptions, there is very little hope in a zombie story. True, some semblance of hope is offered —just to keep the audience engaged—but it's usually yanked away at the end. The most depressing message from these stories is the repeated warning that compassion is a liability. In short, kill Mom-turned-zombie fast, or she will eat you. A softie like me wouldn't last long in a zombie world.

You may be wondering why a person who hates zombies as much as I do is fascinated with zombie films. I've discovered that zombies offer some brilliant parallels to my faith. I see zombies as the unrelenting influence of negative forces in the world—the constant tug of human and spiritual forces out to slowly drive a wedge between me and my Creator.

Interestingly enough, some of the same tactics that help survivors in a zombie apocalypse have helped me in my spiritual struggles. Here are three things I've learned.

1. Sometimes, it's wise to do the opposite of what others are doing.

Survivors in a zombie apocalypse tend to think, act, and look differently than those around them. While others are shrieking and panicking in the streets, the survivors are staying calm and making a plan. While others are throwing an end-of-the-world boozefest, the survivors are locating non-contaminated jugs of water. While others are running into town to empty their bank accounts, the survivors are heading for the hills.

As a Christian, I am also called to be different, to be like Jesus, who constantly does the unexpected—for example, dining at a tax collector's home, talking to a prostitute, and healing those whom others shun. In 1 Peter, the apostle writes to a group of Christians who are being persecuted, advising them on how they should behave. Peter encourages them to stand up for their faith even if they suffer for it. He writes:

> "But you are a chosen race, a royal priesthood, a holy nation, God's own people, in order that you may proclaim the mighty acts of him who called you out of darkness into his marvelous light."[2]

While most North Americans aren't dying for our faith, we may feel like society is moving one way and we are moving another. Our decisions are not determined by whatever everyone else is doing, but by what God tells us is right, just, and holy. We are set apart to be used for God's purposes.

Christians often go against the grain. Sometimes, the difference looks as simple as remaining calm and grounded in our faith when the world around us is losing it. But the most radical act that we can do is to love others. Real love can soften hardened hearts, stunning even our most vicious enemies. It's also the command Jesus gives his disciples before his crucifixion.[3] Loving one another is just as radical in today's age as it was when Jesus first preached it.

2. Fight back strategically.

Sometimes you can't flee. Sometimes, even after you've sought refuge in your remote forest cabin, those pesky zombies still show up. Now you've got the enemy on your doorstep, sticking its dead arm through your screen door, coming after your puppy. What do you do?

You fight back like a honey badger with a fistful of bee larvae.

2 Timothy reminds us: "For God has not given us a spirit of timidity, but of power and love and discipline."[4] We are called to fight for justice, to stand up to bullies and stamp out evil whenever it claws its way through the screen door. And we are also called to fight differently than the world fights, overcoming evil with good. We fight for our hearts and souls, not necessarily our physical bodies. And we don't fight alone.

Scholars aren't sure when David wrote Psalm 27. Perhaps he wrote it before he came to the throne, after defeating a giant with a slingshot. Perhaps it was after the death of his parents. Perhaps it was when he was old and reflecting upon God's faithfulness. Regardless, this psalm is filled with confidence in a God who protects and strengthens.

Even the wicked who try to devour us (like zombies!) are nothing compared to an all-powerful God.[5] David has seen, with his own eyes, the strength of his Lord, and he has learned that seeking after God instead of relying on himself is the best way to fight his enemies.

This doesn't mean we don't think for ourselves. Over and over again in the Bible, God calls us to make wise decisions. We ask questions. We offer love over judgement. We fight strategically. My pastor once told me, "Jesus came to take away our sins, not our brains."

When others try to trap us in the proverbial bee larvae of doom—be it through slick politics or empty philosophies or emotional ideology—we can see those things for what they really are, and expose those lies.

3. Seek shelter and accept help from others.

It can be easy to judge the characters in a zombie movie. From the safety of our living rooms, we can see their obvious mistakes. They're always letting their guards down by standing too close to a window, trapping themselves in a room with no exit, or forgetting the car keys while making a quick escape. They rush in headfirst when they should run, and run when they should fight. After all, that's what makes good TV.

In the movie *Zombieland*, the four main characters are used to fending for themselves. They have managed to stay alive by limiting their attachment to other human beings. Columbia, Tallahassee, Little Rock, and Wichita refuse to even give their real names—only their hometowns. Little by little, however, each member of the group realizes that they need more to survive. They need comfort, love and protection. They slowly let down their guards and become a real family.

It's hard to let down our guards in this world, especially if we've been hurt before. However, God is a ferocious protector and a shelter from life's terrors. Our Creator is entirely worthy of our trust. Psalm 27 reminds us of God's fierce but loving nature, putting our enemies into perspective by comparing them to God's might.

We see a lot of advice in the Bible that suggests we shouldn't be afraid ("Whom should I fear?"[6]). This type of fear isn't referring to the emotional response that you can't control, so don't feel guilty when you panic in the face of a zombie horde. Rather, David is referring to a deliberate choice to trust God's sovereignty and love, even in the face of overwhelming odds against us.

The final verses in the passage talk about waiting for the Lord. We often don't see or understand God's plan. The evils and hurts we face threatens to overwhelm us, and it's difficult to accept that God even cares. Yet, we wait in faith.

Zombie movies depict a desolate world overrun by unrelenting attacks from the undead. There's no place to run, no place to hide. Life seems pretty hopeless. But Psalm 27 is a hopeful reminder that nothing can separate us from the love of God.

Not even a zombie.

Key Scripture

"The Lord is my helper; I will not be afraid. What can anyone do to me?" —Hebrews 13:6

Study Questions

1. What's something you want to do, but it would be wiser to do the opposite?

2. Have you ever been told not to ask questions in church, because that is being "unfaithful?" How does asking questions actually strengthen faith?

3. When have you been tempted to go it alone

instead of relying on God or others for help and shelter?

---

1. *Zombieland*. Directed by Ruben Fleischer. Sony Pictures, 2009.
2. 1 Peter 2:9.
3. John 13:34.
4. 2 Timothy 1:7.
5. Psalm 27:2.
6. Psalm 27:1.

35

A VOICE FROM THE SKY: WONDER IN AN AGE OF SKEPTICISM

BY NATHAN CAMPBELL

"There were many interpretations of Scripture and many interpretations of the natural world... wherever a discrepancy seems to exist, either a scientist or a theologian—maybe both—hasn't been doing [their] job."
—Palmer Joss, *Contact* by Carl Sagan [1]

Read: Psalm 19

Reflect: To categorize Carl Sagan, a scientist and the author of the novel *Contact*, as an outright atheist would be an oversimplification. If painting with a broad brush, Sagan might be categorized with the likes of famous atheists such as Dawkins, Hitchens, or even Douglas Adams. Yet, while Sagan was certainly at odds with organized religion, he would be what Bertrand Russell identifies as a person of science:

"The man of science says 'I think it is so-and-so, but I am not sure.' The man of intellectual curiosity says 'I don't know how it is, but I hope to find out.' The philosophical Skeptic says 'nobody knows and nobody ever can know.'"[2]

Sagan leaves room for the uncertain, unknowable, or yet to be proven, as opposed to outright rejection of divine possibilities.[3]

In *Contact*, the character of Ellie is an archetype familiar to many living in a post-modern society. Her exposure to organized religion causes her to ask well-meaning, thoughtful questions to resolve the apparent conundrums many find in Scripture:

"She was eager for a discussion of these vexing inconsistencies, for an unburdening illumination of God's purpose."

Yet, as happens all too often in the real world, Ellie finds herself in the company of religious leaders who are either unable or unwilling to thoughtfully answer her questions, leaving her to conclude that "wild horses wouldn't drag her to another Bible class."

Interestingly, Ellie does not reject the sacred or holy; rather, she finds them in the natural world:

"Theologians seem to have a special aspect of the feeling of the sacred or holy. They call it 'numinous'... and the human response to it is 'absolute astonishment.'"

Numinous, according to C.S. Lewis, "may be described as awe, and the object which excites it as the Numinous."[4]

As an adult, Ellie discovers a "voice from the sky" in the form of a radio signal from the vicinity of the star Vega. This transmission is later dubbed "the Message." Debate erupts among both scientists and clergy over the origin and purpose of the Message.

Ellie, a skeptic, is not incapable of numinous awe, which she demonstrates in response to the Message. Her application of science and the wonders it reveals is where she finds the sacred, stating:

> "If that's what religious people talk about when they use words like *sacred* or *holy*, I'm with them. I felt something like that just in listening for a signal, never mind in actually receiving it. I think all of science elicits that awe."

A sense of the numinous in the natural world is neither unavailable nor unknown to us. Psalms 19:1 reads, "The heavens are telling the glory of God; and the firmament proclaims his handiwork." This psalm, written by David, explores the beauty of God's creation. We *should* be in awe of nature, the difference is in the attribution. Nature's glory reflects the Creator's glory. Ellie finds meaning in the mere act of listening for a message from beyond. In the sacred experience of listening for the voice of God through prayer, so, too, do we find the sacred.

In his book *Miracles*, C.S. Lewis states:

"Nothing can seem extraordinary until you have discovered what is ordinary. Belief in miracles, far from depending on an ignorance of the laws of nature, is only possible in so far as those laws are known."[5]

The goal of science, then, is to determine the laws of nature. This is necessary to both the skeptic's and the Christian's sense of wonder, for the numinous may be found even in the depth of 'ordinary' complexities.

Ellie is an honest observer, capable of admitting this innate need:

"Look, we all have a thirst for wonder. It's a deeply human quality. Science and religion are both bound up with it. What I'm saying is, you don't have to make stories up, you don't have to exaggerate. There's wonder enough in the real world. Nature's a lot better at inventing wonders than we are."

Her statement is the turning point of the "cosmic irony" that carries Ellie from skeptic to prophet. Ellie becomes a Pauline figure in the story, because she has a transformative experience, much like Saul on the road to Damascus in Acts 9:3–19. She is traveling on a road (in this case, a wormhole), takes a baptism-like swim in an otherworldly ocean, and encounters an extraterrestrial being of extraordinary power and wisdom. Ellie is metaphorically reborn as a result of this experience, and she returns with no evidence. She is now in the same position as those she once accused of making up stories and exaggerating. Cosmic irony, indeed.

Ellie's former compatriots feel she is lying and manipulating the situation for some ill gain or perverse pleasure. She is now in the role of a reluctant, but resolute, prophet, obliged to speak the truth about her experience. The only person who believes her story is a man of faith, Palmer Joss, who "listened sympathetically, intelligently, and indeed generously." Ellie is now an apostle, a messenger relating personal experiences that are nearly impossible to prove but espousing truths about the existence of the Numinous.

If the heavens display God's glory, do they need our stalwart defense of their origin? Should we rather not be patient with those who doubt? As a grieving father said to Jesus, "I believe; help my unbelief!"[6]

Our universe is not one of fantasy and imagination, but a tangible one we can see, touch, measure, and, most importantly, marvel at. Skeptics and believers alike share a common ground: wonder. Wonder is a bridge on which we can meet. We can crane our necks and gaze into the vastness in awe of the beauty of the moon, the stars, the nebulae, the unknown, the unknowable, the Numinous... together.

Key Scripture

"The voice of the Lord is over the waters; the God of glory thunders, the Lord, over mighty waters. The voice of the Lord is powerful; the voice of the Lord is full of majesty." —Psalm 29:3–4

Study Questions

1. How do you think science and faith are related? Have you had doubts about either?

2. How have you handled interactions with agnostic or atheist friends or family? What common ground do you share in regards to the numinous?

3. What would it look like to listen "sympathetically, intelligently, and generously" to someone who challenges your fundamental beliefs?

---

1. Sagan, Carl. *Contact*. Simon and Schuster, 1985.
2. Russell, Bertrand. *A History of Western Philosophy*. Simon and Schuster, 1945.
3. Sagan, Carl. *The Demon-Haunted World: Science as a Candle in the Dark*. Random House, 1995.
4. Lewis, C.S. *The Problem of Pain*. The Centenary Press, 1940.
5. Lewis, C.S. *Miracles*. London & Glasgow: Collins/Fontana, 1947.
6. Mark 9:24.

36

FINAL FANTASY VIII AND THE PROMISE THAT WE ARE NOT ALONE

BY LESTER LIAO

"I'll be waiting for you. If you come here, you'll find me. I promise."
　　—Squall Leonhart, *Final Fantasy VIII*[1]

Read: Joshua 1:1–9

Reflect: In the role-playing video game *Final Fantasy VIII*, Squall Leonhart is a lone wolf whose journey leads to friendship and the salvation of the world. But his upbringing is dark. He grows up in an orphanage, and even there loses the one sisterly figure close to him. Throughout the game, players see flashbacks of Squall weeping alone in the rain, resolving to make it through life on his own.

But, as his story progresses, Squall finds himself embroiled in a cosmic conflict, and he needs help. Zell, Selphie, and Quistis rescue him from an electrocution torture chamber, Irvine helps him recover his lost childhood memories, and all of Balamb Garden (the mercenary group he trains with) help him to fight against the Galbadian army. In a moment of lucidity, he realizes that self sufficiency is a fantasy.

In the midst of this chaos, Rinoa, a member of a group of freedom fighters who joins forces with Squall, becomes the primary vehicle for his redemption. As Squall struggles to understand his own reservations toward others and the fear of rejection that drives his independence, Rinoa reminds him that relying on another is not a weakness, but a strength.

Squall's desire for independence is familiar. I want to stand out in a crowd, pursue my dreams, and free myself from the bonds of social obligation. It's what I've come to value in a chaotic world. I turn to myself as God. But I am left unsatisfied, and I remember God's way is lifegiving. Mutual dependence with others fosters the relationships that make life whole.

Squall lives in the shadow of abandonment, and he's afraid of becoming attached to anyone. He is well on his way to the "unbreakable, impenetrable, irredeemable" heart that C.S. Lewis warns of in *The Four Loves*. Lewis writes that if we continuously refuse others into our lives because we're afraid of pain or disappointment, our hearts will grow cold and eventually petrify.

When Rinoa and Squall speak on the evening of the concert at Balamb Garden, he tells her, "I don't want friends who won't be around tomorrow." Squall walls people off because he's afraid they'll abandon him. He tells Ellone, a woman who transports his consciousness through time and relies on him to change the past,

"Don't... Don't count on me." His hard heart keeps him from seeing that she is the very sisterly figure he lost in his childhood.

But perfect love casts out fear.[2] The incarnation of Christ fights the lie I harbour in my heart alongside Squall —that I will be alone.

Does God leave me when it hurts most? After his wife died, C.S. Lewis wrestled with this question in *A Grief Observed*. He wondered if God cared. He felt like God slammed the door in his face when he was most desperate. In losing Ellone, Squall feels similarly abandoned and utterly alone. It is the pain of loss compounded by a look of indifference from the one who is supposed to make things right.

God invites us to use this space for lament and wonder. Jesus reminds me that he, too, was alone. His divine pain brings him to sit with me as the tears flow. He is not a detached onlooker, but one who also feels loss. And there I begin to find comfort. I may not know all the answers, but I do know the Creator cares.

The God who goes to the cross is not a God who slams the door. God is there regardless of what my feelings are telling me, and God has taken the first step to meet me. This kind of love is at work in Rinoa, who takes the initiative to be vulnerable and to care about Squall despite his rebuffs. Over time, his heart of stone is transformed into a heart of flesh.

In the game, the party comes face to face with the possibility of being lost in time, and their lives are on the line. This is when Squall tells Rinoa that he will be there for her.

This is what love does. It reminds us that we are not alone.

Despite a culture that prizes convenience and minimal obligations, love compels us to make these promises to each other—I will be there. I will love you. I will not abandon you. Our promises pour forth as acts of sacrifice, placing another's need ahead of our own convenience.

This is precisely what God does for us. God's promises are not based on austere obligation. Indeed, God makes promises out of love, and through that love, we are transformed. Just as Rinoa's love transforms Squall, God's love enables us to love.

In Joshua 1:1–9, the Israelites have lost Moses, and they are preparing to cross the Jordan River. Joshua assumes command, and he is faced with the enormous task of leading the people into a foreign land without his mentor. This is when God makes a promise. When life seems insurmountable and the future uncertain, God reminds Joshua that he is not alone. God's words speak directly to Joshua's apprehension (and my own). Do not be frightened. Do not be dismayed. God knows my heart. And God knows I need a guiding word and constant presence.

For Squall and company, the fantastical dimensions of time warps and space combat exacerbate the uncertainty they face. But Squall's promise to Rinoa is an anchor in the storm. It says, regardless of what happens, *this* will stay true.

Similarly, God's promises ground us. In binding myself to God and to others through community, I create a framework for my life that upholds me through trials.

God's promise of divine presence in the face of life's pain and challenges are mirrored in the community of friends who become the body of Christ. When I stumble, I know they will be there.

Christ is the ultimate promise, the unchanging declaration of love, the Emmanuel, God with us. God's promises have changed my life forever. When I'm tempted to hide my heartache like Squall, love invades my soul, and the relationship makes me a new creation. And if I ever find myself adrift, whether floating in space or on the Island Closest to Hell, those promises stand forever.

Key Scripture

"There is no fear in love, but perfect love casts out fear; for fear has to do with punishment, and whoever fears has not reached perfection in love. We love because he first loved us."
—1 John 4:18–19

Study Questions

1. When do you most doubt the promises of God? Is this doubt a manifestation of fear, like Squall's?

2. Do you hold off from making promises to other people? Why or why not?

3. How might Squall's journey to find community encourage you to build greater trust in God?

1. *Final Fantasy VIII*. PlayStation, Square, 1999.
2. John 4:18.

37

A FATHER BY ANY OTHER NAME

BY EMMA SKRUMEDA

John Silver: "Your father's not the teaching sort?"
Jim Hawkins: "No, he was more the 'taking off and never coming back' sort."
—*Treasure Planet*[1]

Read: Genesis 1:26–27

Reflect: When the musical montage in *Treasure Planet* begins, I know it's time to break out the tissues. If you've seen the film, which is Disney's 2002 animated take on *Treasure Island*, you know exactly what part I'm talking about.

Jim Hawkins, a teenager aboard the spacecraft *R.L.S. Legacy*, is in search of fortune and adventure. He's also under the reluctant tutelage of the half-robot pirate John Silver. The scenes flip between various nautical tasks—knot-tying, dish-washing, scraping barnacles from the hull—and moments from Jim's past. It's here that the water-works start.

We see Jim as a little boy, excitedly showing a toy boat to his father, only to be brushed aside; Jim, a few years old, waking up to his mother crying in the kitchen, father heading out the door for a waiting ship; and Jim sprinting after his Dad, making it to the end of the dock just as the ship takes off. It's here that you start to understand why Jim enters into a tenuous father-son relationship with John Silver. Even though Jim doesn't trust Silver (since Silver acts suspiciously and, earlier, Jim was given a warning about a cyborg), he wants a father figure in his life. The problem is he doesn't know what a healthy version of that relationship looks like.

I've always been close with my dad, something I become more grateful for the older I get. As a kid, I didn't think about our relationship as anything special. Of course my dad would be at my piano recital, would coach my soccer team, would read bedtime stories to me and my brothers. It was a given that he loved me and wanted the best for me. So when people referred to God as a father, I understood, unconsciously, that this meant God was loving, fair, and safe. It was a metaphor that landed the way it was supposed to, and one that could accurately inform my faith and draw me closer to God.

But my experience of a present and caring father is not a universal one.

"Ever since his father left... well, Jim just never recovered," says Sarah Hawkins in *Treasure Planet*.

What does "father" mean to Jim Hawkins? Cold. Distant. Indifferent. Someone who will hurt you. Someone who will leave you. These associations are not easily forgotten or ignored, and they represent deep and lasting pain rather than unconditional love. Jim's intrinsic understanding of "God the Father" would likely be different from mine.

There's an old story about three blind people who touch a different part of an elephant. "An elephant is like a tree," says one, feeling a sturdy leg. "An elephant is like a broom," says another as they are swatted by the hanging tail. "An elephant is like a palm frond," says the last, stroking the wide expanse of an ear. All of them are correct, yet each description is too limited to fully convey the reality of an elephant.

The way we think about God is no different. In the Psalms, David writes that God has "greatness that no one can fathom,"[2] and he spends the entire chapter trying to describe the extent of God's majesty. Even his beautiful poetry does not come close to conveying the true magnitude of God, because the Creator is far beyond our understanding. Our human terms for God are, by necessity, metaphor—and they all fall short of God's true, indescribable, nature. While using "Father" and male pronouns to talk about God isn't inaccurate, using *only* those terms is limiting ourselves to a single facet of God's identity.

The idea of describing God in non-masculine terms is neither new nor unbiblical. Even in Bible translations that use male pronouns and titles for God, there are frequent scriptural depictions of God as feminine and maternal. God is called a "mother hen;"[3] an "eagle gathering her chicks under her wings;"[4] a mother experiencing labour pains;[5] the mistress of a household;[6] and "the one who gave [us] birth."[7] These concepts have existed since the very beginning of the Church.

In 1373, Julian of Norwich, a medieval Christian mystic (coincidentally, the woman who inspired my middle name) wrote in her *Revelations of Divine Love*: "God rejoices that He is our Father, and God rejoices that He is our Mother."[8] I love this quote because it invites me to ascribe to God the qualities that I associate with the word *maternal*, and assures me that not only will God be okay with that, but that She will find joy in it. God is gentle, comforting, intimate, emotional, and fiercely protective.[9] She delights in these aspects of our relationship.

Comparing God to a mother might allow someone like Jim Hawkins to encounter God free from the specter of an absent father. Though Jim's relationship with Silver does demonstrate flashes of what a healthy child-parent relationship should look like, it is generally painful and ends with them going their separate ways. Jim's journey in *Treasure Planet* is, ultimately, about his own self-confidence and learning that he is neither trapped by his past failings nor doomed to be a disappointment. But his experience with father figures remains tarnished. It may be that God the Mother, reflecting the tenacious love of his own mother, would give him something more familiar to connect with. He might find it easier to reflect on God's nature this way.

Of course, people also have complicated relationships with their mothers. Using varied language and labels to describe God offers different avenues for us to approach our Creator; those who cannot intuitively connect with "God the Father" may find much more comfort and understanding from another concept. We also broaden our understanding of who God is with the variety of metaphors found in the Bible. How does our perception change by considering God a mother, a parent, a creator, a holy spirit, a saviour, a light, a fire, a rock, a potter, a shepherd, a loaf of bread, a vine, a shield? How might using a variety of pronouns—"He" to represent the masculine metaphors in the Bible, "She" to represent the feminine descriptors, and "They" to represent the aspects of Their identity that may be neither feminine nor masculine—encourage us to see God in a new light?

Widening our metaphorical language for God helps us to comprehend more aspects of divinity. The very act of trying to consider God from all angles gives us a glimpse at how undefinable God is, and how exciting it is to understand even a small piece of Their being.

It is remarkable that we humans are made after God's image when Their identity is so vast. When I talk about God using feminine terms, or hear others reference Her in that way, I am viscerally reminded of the ways that God is reflected in me. When I think about God as fire, I grow in my understanding of how He purifies, like flames sterilizing the edge of a knife. When I picture God as a shepherd, I feel seen, and loved unconditionally; it is this image, more than almost any other, which communicates to me the lengths that They will go to to find me, and care for me, and protect me from harm.

Opening our conceptualization of God invites us into a deeper understanding of Them, removes obstacles which may keep some from ever connecting with Her, and invites countless others into intimate communion with a God they embody. Our faith can be enriched by considering God as vast and multi-faceted, not limited to one gender or identity.

Key Passage

> "As a mother comforts her child, so I will comfort you." —Isaiah 66:13

Study Questions

1. How does the suggestion to refer to God as the feminine "Her" or the gender-neutral "They" make you feel? Be honest with yourself and sit with those feelings, especially if the thought creates discomfort. Try and get to the root of those emotions, and figure out why you feel the way you do.

2. How would referring to God as "Mother" or "Parent" rather than "Father" influence your perception of Them?

3. Reflect on some of the other titles ascribed to God—shepherd, monarch, teacher, etc. What does each term tell you about God's nature? Come up with some of your own metaphorical descriptions of God that speak to you of who They are.

---

1. *Treasure Planet.* Directed by Ron Clements and John Musker. Buena Vista Pictures, 2002.
2. Psalm 145:3.
3. Matthew 23:37 and Luke 13:34.
4. Deuteronomy 32:11.
5. Isaiah 42:14.
6. Psalm 123:2–3.

7. Deuteronomy 21:18.
8. Julian of Norwich. *Revelations of Divine Love*. Penguin Books, 1999 (originally published 1670).
9. Of course, these qualities are not unique to mothers, nor are they present in all mothers. These are just some of the associations that I, personally, make with the terms *mother* and *maternal*.

38

SOLOMON'S METHOD TO "LIVE LONG AND PROSPER"

BY ROBERT WHITE

T'Pau: "Live long and prosper, Spock." / **Spock:** "I shall do neither. I have killed my captain and my friend."
—*Star Trek: the Original Series*[1]

Read: Ecclesiastes 4:9–12

Reflect: "Amok Time" is a fan-favourite episode from *Star Trek: The Original Series* due to the backstory about our favourite Vulcan, but the part that spoke most to me was the incredible friendship between three of my favourite characters: First Officer Spock, Captain James T. Kirk, and Dr. Leonard McCoy.

In the episode, Spock behaves strangely, exhibiting outbursts of emotion. He reroutes the ship to Vulcan without Kirk's approval, then claims to not remember doing so when Kirk confronts him. In the *Enterprise*'s sick bay, McCoy notes that Spock is experiencing physical and emotional stress, and Spock admits he's going through *pon farr*, a "blood fever" that occurs periodically in Vulcan males. Spock must return to his home planet and mate with his fiancée, T'Pring, or die.

Kirk disobeys Starfleet orders to bring Spock to Vulcan. When they arrive, Spock asks Kirk and McCoy to join him for the wedding ceremony. To the Vulcans, Spock's friendship with these humans is unusual; due to their devotion to logic and cultural differences, Vulcans have a history of seeing themselves "above" humans. As a team aboard the *Enterprise*, however, the three characters have learned to appreciate their differences and work together.

T'Pring arrives with Stonn, a pureblood Vulcan, whom she prefers to Spock, and tells Spock she has opted for the *kal-if-fee*, a challenge between Spock and a champion of her choice. Then she surprises everyone by choosing Kirk to fight for her instead of Stonn. Kirk accepts the challenge before he learns that it's to the death. Spock is dismayed at the idea of killing his friend, but cannot deny his culture's tradition. The two fight, and the challenge ends when Spock garrottes Kirk and McCoy declares Kirk dead. With the blood fever gone, Spock releases T'Pring from their marriage.

While there are some negative connotations to this story, including the implication that T'Pring is property (one of the many examples of the objectification of women for which *Star Trek: The Original Series* has been justifiably criticized), "Amok Time" demonstrates the depth of friendship that's developed between Spock, Kirk, and McCoy. Theirs is a friendship that echoes the words of Ecclesiastes: "And though one might prevail against another, two will withstand one. A threefold cord is not quickly broken."[2]

Ecclesiastes, likely authored by King Solomon, is written in a world-weary, regretful tone. The book starts off with Solomon, the wisest and richest man in the world, listing all his accomplishments, wisdom, riches, possessions, wives, and concubines. But all these things add up to a great big zero, says Solomon. He refers to his power, possessions, and accomplishments as "chasing after wind,"[3] notes how the righteous often get what the wicked deserve,[4] and says dreaming about nice things is meaningless.[5]

But then, sandwiched between these outpourings of lamentation are the occasional nuggets of wisdom, like this one: "Two are better than one, because they have a good reward for their toil."[6] Solomon spends a paragraph pointing out the value of community, and it's curious why he pauses abruptly to talk about friendship. The implications are clear: there is no joy in being a selfish, bitter, lonely person. Be kind, love your neighbour, and find community instead.

Notably, this isn't the only place in the Bible that discusses this topic. From Naomi and Ruth's friendship, to Jesus' disciples spreading the word of Christ, to the covenant between David and Jonathan, stories about community abound. "It is not good that the man should be alone," God says in Genesis 2:18. "We, who are many, are one body in Christ," Paul writes in Romans 12:5.

Despite our familiarity with these stories, it's easy to build walls around ourselves. After all, who knows who might hurt us if we let them in. Plus, we might have to share our wealth, time, expertise, or emotional support, and that sounds like too much work. North American society particularly values self-sufficiency; look out for number one, and don't ask for help because you should be able to do everything yourself. But, as Christians, we are encouraged to support one another, to use our different gifts as a team, to offer each other grace and companionship.

Perhaps Solomon made a selfish choice during his life —the wrong choice—and that's why he goes out of his way to lament about how wealth and solitude are meaningless. Maybe he saw many others making selfish choices during his long lifetime. His advice speaks to the importance of community—something Kirk understands intimately.

Kirk could have kept his career (and himself) safe if he had followed Starfleet's command and hadn't gone to Vulcan. But his friendship with Spock means more to him than any selfish desires. He puts himself in harm's way for his friend. And, as Spock returns his friendship, he is devastated when he thinks he's killed Kirk.

Of course, Kirk isn't really dead. Upon returning to the *Enterprise*, McCoy explains that some medical trickery allowed Kirk to appear dead, giving Spock the needed victory. McCoy's quick thinking saved both Kirk's life and the trio's enduring friendship.

It can be easy to get tired with life and tempting to make the choices that benefit us, and us alone. But God is a relational God. Like it or not, we are made to be part of a family, motivated by love instead of selfishness, bound by peace.

It is relationships such as these that, unlike any treasures or accomplishments in the world, allow us to "live long and prosper."

Key Scripture

> "Now you are the body of Christ and individually members of it." —1 Corinthians 12:27

Study Questions

1. In "Amok Time," Spock shares details about Vulcan mating ritual with Kirk, information that is normally kept private. Why is it important to have someone with whom you can share the intimate details of your life?

2. What are the practical benefits of friendship that Solomon lists in Ecclesiastes? Do any of these surprise you?

3. How are you better able to serve God as part of a community than on your own?

---

1. *Star Trek: The Original Series.* "Amok Time," season 2, episode 1. Directed by Joseph Pevney. CBS Television, 1967.
2. Ecclesiastes 4:12.
3. Ecclesiastes 4:14.
4. Ecclesiastes 8:14.
5. Ecclesiastes 6:9.
6. Ecclesiastes 4:9.

39

FIGHTING THE GOOD FIGHT: CONFLICT IN THE GOSPELS AND ASIMOV'S FOUNDATION

BY TIM WEBSTER

"Violence is the last refuge of the incompetent"
—Salvor Hardin, *Foundation* by Isaac Asimov [1]

Read: John 4:1–42

Reflect: Isaac Asimov once mentioned he didn't understand why his Foundation books were popular, because nothing happens. He was being ironic, of course, and the statement is both exquisitely true and decidedly untrue.

Good stories hinge on conflict, and there is plenty to be found in Asimov's tales of a fallen galactic empire, the ensuing chaos, and the embryonic growth of not only a new, but a new kind of empire crafted by the fledgling science of "psychohistory." The Foundation series, however, is not rife with rugged, faster-than-light starships, laser battles, or slavering monsters. The protagonists are not the dashing, derring-do, self-sufficient daredevils that inhabit other science-fiction franchises. Instead, these individuals foresee and meet conflict with wit, wisdom, and grace.

I confess: I wish I was more like Asimov's characters. I don't meet every conflict in my life with wit, wisdom, and grace; in fact, if we're in traffic and you were to cut me off, neglect to signal your intention, or flick your cigarette butt out the window (you litterbug!), I would probably express indiscretion, foolishness, and judgement.

These are the kinds of reactions that lead to more sin and trouble in the world, and they are certainly not the example Jesus sets. As I read the Gospels, I see that Jesus engages with every conflict that arises and deals with it directly. He challenges the traditions of the religious, the assumptions of sinners, the authority of leaders, and the powers of darkness everywhere he goes and with everything he says. From the moment of his birth to his ascension into Heaven, Jesus' life and ministry are full of conflict, and he meets each one with wit, wisdom, and grace—and only once with violence.

Some suggest that the Jesus who blesses the peacemakers, tells us to turn the other cheek, encourages us to bless those who curse us and love our enemies is avoiding conflict, but I disagree. In order to exhibit these qualities, you must be engaged in some sort of conflict! Like it or not, you are in conflict with someone who hits you; you are in conflict with someone who curses you; you are in conflict with an enemy. If you want to be a peacemaker, you have to wade into the midst of a conflict. Jesus himself said: "I didn't come to bring peace, but a sword."[2]

In the creation story, "God separated the light from the darkness."[3] Even this is conflict. The pattern continues as creation unfolds: earth and sky, land and sea, plants emerging through soil, animals consuming plants, until finally, the creation of humans. Conflict is knit into the very fabric of our being—we cannot move, breathe, eat, or *exist* unless two muscles in our bodies pull in opposite directions.

The universe is founded on conflict: protons and electrons, atmosphere and vacuum. At this very moment, you are in conflict with the force of gravity (unless you happen to be on the International Space Station). As you age, your ability to manage that conflict may decline. If, however, you deliberately engage with that conflict, daily, with a consistent regimen of what we call "exercise," you will better be able to manage that conflict. In fact, if you don't engage the never-ending conflict with gravity, you will never get anywhere; you will die of your own infected bedsores.

So, if conflict is a fundamental, God-designed, necessary, even desirable force in the universe, then why do we so consistently avoid it? Perhaps we're turned off by the many negative outcomes of poorly-managed conflicts: hurt feelings, anger, broken relationships, violence, abuse. Taken to their ultimate conclusion, poorly-managed conflicts lead to war and all of its attendant horrors. Avoiding pain and suffering is understandable, but when we avoid all conflict at all costs—to the detriment of those around us, our own souls, and our individual and collective faith—we are ignoring Christ's example.

Conflict is not the same thing as violence. Conflict enables progress and growth; it provides traction, enabling things to move forward, in relationships and with physics.

Within Asimov's series, the nascent Foundation experiences so-called "Seldon Crises" at key points of its fore-ordained history, as some floundering bit of the old empire heaves in the opposite direction of the new Foundation. During these crises, certain factions within the Foundation rise up and noisily attempt to retain power and control, even suggesting taking up arms and going to war. During one such conflict, Mayor Hober Mallow wins a three-year war without a single shot being fired, resulting in the enlargement of both the territory and influence of the Foundation.

Jesus similarly grows the kingdom of Heaven.When he encounters a Samaritan woman at a well in John 4, Jesus is hot, tired, and thirsty, so he asks the woman for a drink. She can't believe he'd even speak to her and is prepared to refuse him on that basis alone. He persists, not by lambasting or pressuring her, but simply by telling the truth: about himself, about her, about the kingdom of Heaven. By the time he is done not only is the woman a believer, but so are many others in that town.

Healthy, well-managed conflicts are not about "winning" or "losing," and if that becomes the focus, they are poorly-managed conflicts and, no matter the outcome, both parties have already lost. Healthy conflicts build community instead of tearing it down. This is why God has knit conflict into the fabric of the universe, into our very selves. It's supposed to draw us together, but like every other good gift our Creator gave, we've subverted it... and avoided it.

The purpose of the Foundation is to compress 30,000 years of chaotic lawlessness following the collapse of the

Galactic Empire into a single millennium, guided by the wisdom of the Seldon Plan. The plan prepares them for conflict. Seldon, however, is wise enough to know that he doesn't know enough, and he arranges for his successors to manage and nurture the plan after his passing and well into the future.

Before he leaves, Jesus reminds his disciples that he is the Messiah and tasks them with building his Church. If we are to follow Jesus' example as we accept this awesome responsibility, then we, too—like the Foundation—must prepare for conflict. You can't bind or loose anything through avoidance; you must engage. *Winning* (being right) and *losing* (being wrong) are irrelevant; *engaging* is everything, because doing so makes a space for community.

Key Scripture

"I'm giving you the keys to the kingdom; whatever you bind on earth will be bound in Heaven, and whatever you loose on earth will be loosed in Heaven." —Matthew 16:19

Study Questions

1. What conflicts are you avoiding and why?

2. Can you see ways to meet regularly occurring conflicts in your life with wit, wisdom, and grace?

3. How can you ask God to prepare you to engage in healthy conflicts?

_____

1. Asimov, Isaac. *Foundation*. Gnome Press, 1951.
2. Matthew 10:34.
3. Genesis 1:4.

40

TRUST, SURRENDER, AND DIRK GENTLY

BY JARED AND NATHAN SIEBERT

"Everything is connected. But only I can see it. I'm not psychic. But I am... something. When I was young, I would get... intuitions about things, little hunches about the way the universe worked... It was like reading in another language, like signs with symbols I didn't understand."

—Dirk Gently, *Dirk Gently's Holistic Detective Agency*[1]

Read: Hebrews 11

Reflect: Have you ever wondered what it would have been like to be one of Jesus' disciples while he was on Earth? Perhaps you see yourself as the only disciple who wasn't afraid during the storm at sea, or as the one who denies Jesus out of fear, or as the one who dreams of being at Jesus' right hand in Heaven. To read the Gospels is to come face to face with human frailty, arrogance, and cowardice. It is also to come face to face with the awesome power of faith at work in the world. Whichever way you approach the stories, you leave your time in the Gospels asking, "What do I do with Jesus now? Here? With the amount that I currently understand?"

The Bible is full of stories about people following God's instructions without fully understanding the Creator's plans. Abraham must set out from his people before he can understand where he is going.[2] Mary must allow herself to be part of God's plan before she understands how it is even possible.[3] Each of the disciples responds to Jesus' call to follow before they know where they are going.[4] This is what 19th century Christian Philosopher Soren Kierkegaard refers to as the "leap of faith."[5]

Driven by the big questions of human experience, we often find ourselves at the end of reason and rationality. Reason and rationality, while helpful guides and powerful gifts from God, can not always take us the entire journey. Sometimes the journey requires that we step out in faith in order to press deeper. As Kiekegaard suggests, life can only be understood backwards, but it must be lived forwards.[6] The world of *Dirk Gently's Holistic Detective Agency* follows similar logic. The show's mystery can only be understood backwards, but it must be solved by living forward.

Each character in the show must surrender some element of control in their lives if they are to, as Bart and Dirk say, become "like a leaf floating on the stream of creation."[7] The secret of Bart's abilities as an assassin and Dirk's abilities as a detective is their respective capacity to go wherever events lead them. The same goes for their companions. Each companion slowly starts to believe that

Bart and Dirk will be in the right spot at the right time. As their faith grows, so does their level of participation in solving the case. This level of surrender is no small feat and costs each character something unique.

Dirk must surrender his control over whether people like him and, ultimately, his hope of ever having friends:

> "I don't have any friends. I am always surrounded by bizarre and frightening states of disaster, and I am always alone. Even you keep saying you're not my friend. But since you're the closest thing I've had, I'd really appreciate it if you'd stop calling yourself an a**hole."[8]

Todd, another of the show's main characters and Dirk's companion, must surrender his desire for control if he hopes to remain part of the story. He has a need to understand what is going on and is afraid people will discover his past lies and misdeeds. As he grows closer to Dirk, Todd learns to rely more and more on Dirk's ability to follow events as they unfold and to release his need for control.

It is only when Todd finally trusts his friends and reveals his secrets that he begins to see the interconnectedness of the universe, and only then can he take charge and brave the unknown. Similarly, our faith as Christians is influenced by the people who surround us, people who keep us in check and journey with us.

The characters push each other in ways that challenge what they know, what they believe about the universe, and, ultimately, what their own purpose is. Todd finds himself in a story he wants nothing to do with, but he can't ignore it as his friends push him toward the truth. We need people to lift us up when we're down and to challenge us when we're getting ahead of ourselves. This type of vulnerability requires us to give up something of ourselves—often, our pride and fear—to be faithful.

As the writer of Hebrews reminds us, "Faith is the assurance of things hoped for, the conviction of things not seen."[9] As we read the entire chapter, we come to realize this isn't an isolated case. Faith is fundamental to being the people of God, and we have always wrestled with its challenge. From Cain and Abel to the present, faith is fundamental to solving the case.

The people of God are called "foreigners and strangers on earth"[10] for a reason. Even though we come from the dust of the earth, even though we are born here, even though we continue to live here, we live as though we are strangers. Following God can put us at odds with life as usual or as expected. Like the characters in *Dirk Gently's Holistic Detective Agency*, as we get caught up in the unfolding story of the universe, we find our world is comprehensible only to other people of faith. To everyone else it appears to be madness and chaos. That is why the life of faith requires, well, faith.

Jesus warns us that following him could mean losing family, money, respect, and even our own lives. Who in their right minds would agree to such an offer? The Bible refers to the ongoing process of following Jesus as dying,[11] denying ourselves and picking up our cross.[12] While not all of us give up the exact same things or give them up in the exact same order, we are required to surrender if we want to say with our lives that "Jesus is Lord." This type of faith doesn't mean we can't ask questions or revise our understanding of what following Jesus means. Life with God is immense, complex, and, oftentimes, beyond our understanding. Faith is how we navigate the territory of knowing and loving God.

Dirk Gently's Holistic Detective Agency gives us a unique look at what a life of faith requires. As the story unfolds in all its absurd and paradoxical beauty, it requires acts of faith from its characters and even from its audience: you must have faith that this show is actually heading somewhere! You must believe that, as the pieces fall into place, it will all make sense. If you have the patience, the show pays off in many delightful ways. The same can be said of life with Jesus.

Key Scripture

"Jesus said to him, 'Have you believed because you have seen me? Blessed are those who have not seen and yet have come to believe.'"
—John 20:29

Study Questions

1. What are areas of control you struggle to give up? How can you let go of that desire for control in order to trust that the end will reveal the trajectory of the plot?

2. Who are the people that have played a significant role in who you are today? What role does the

community of faith play in your capacity to trust the unknown?

3. What are you holding on to, perhaps out of pride or fear, that might be interfering with your access to trust?

---

1. *Dirk Gently's Holistic Detective Agency*. "Very Erectus," season 1, episode 5. Directed by Tamra Davis. BBC, 2016.
2. Genesis 12:1–3.
3. Luke 1:34–38.
4. Matthew 4:18–22, Mark 3:16–20, Luke 5:1–11.
5. Kierkegaard, Søren. *Fear and Trembling*. Penguin, 1986 (originally published 1843).
6. This is a common paraphrase of his original statement from *The Journals of Søren Kierkegaard* (IV A 164), 1843: "It is perfectly true, as the philosophers say, that life must be understood backwards. But they forget the other proposition, that it must be lived forwards."
7. *Dirk Gently's Holistic Detective Agency*. "Lost & Found," season 1, episode 2. Directed by Dean Parisot. BBC, 2016.
8. *Dirk Gently's Holistic Detective Agency*. "Very Erectus," season 1, episode 5. Directed by Tamra Davis. BBC, 2016.
9. Hebrews 11:1.
10. Hebrews 11:13.
11. Galatians 2:20.
12. Luke 9:23.

41

FRINGE SCIENCE, IDENTITY, AND FREE WILL

BY ALLISON ALEXANDER

"Must be nice to know who you are. To know your place in the world."
—Peter Bishop, *Fringe*[1]

Read: Exodus 34:1–8

Reflect: Have you ever wondered what your life would look like if you'd made different choices in the past? This is one of the many questions explored by *Fringe*, a TV series that follows FBI agent Olivia Dunham as she works with an institutionalized scientist, Walter Bishop, and his son, Peter Bishop, to solve supernatural mysteries. Many of these strange occurrences in the world are linked to the cracks between two universes—our universe and a parallel version that Walter travelled to when Peter was a boy.

This parallel universe is based on the multiverse theory—that there are multiple universes based on every possible reality. In effect, with every decision you make, an alternate reality exists where you made a different choice;

those choices, and the choices of people around you, may influence you to become a different person. And the very world you live in might also look different.

In *Fringe*, the parallel universe is fairly similar to ours, but it has many small differences: their technology is more advanced, they use airships for travel, the Statue of Liberty is bronze, the World Trade Center is still standing, and popular culture is different (for starters, Peter reads a comic about the Red Lantern, and *Back to the Future* stars Eric Stoltz. Also, when you're visiting New York City, make you sure you see that hit musical, *Dogs*).

One of the most fascinating parts of the show is when characters meet their doppelgangers from the other universe. Olivia's counterpart, "Fauxlivia," is a red-head who is more outgoing and relaxed; their differences are largely due to Olivia's mom dying but Fauxlivia's mom surviving—Olivia experienced a childhood of abuse from her stepfather as a result. Walter's counterpart, "Walternate," is ruthless and cruel; their differences are mostly because Walter has brain damage and Walternate does not. Also, Walternate was never friends with William Bell, a significant character in Walter's life, because Bell died as a child in the parallel universe. Lincoln Lee's counterpart (Walter doesn't give Alternate Lincoln Lee one of those delightful nicknames, so we'll just call him "Lee") is more outgoing, arrogant, and confident than Lincoln; interestingly enough, the differences in their personalities don't have an explanation.

In Season Four, the two Lincolns work a case together. Lincoln has noticed their obvious differences—he is shy and reserved while Lee tends to take the spotlight. The two discuss where their paths may have diverged, but can't pinpoint any major differences in their lives. Their child-hoods, right down to their tenth grade science teacher, were the same.

> **Lincoln:** "Which leads me back to why. Our lives seemed pretty parallel, but somewhere along the line, we became very different people."
> **Lee:** "Maybe it's free will. I don't buy that we're all just defined by our circumstances. Maybe I just made a choice to become the man I wanted to be."[2]

In Exodus 34, Moses climbs Mount Sinai for a second time to receive a new set of the Ten Commandments inscribed on stone tablets (he broke the first tablets because the Israelites decided to worship a golden calf instead of God—see Exodus 32).

God speaks to Moses on the mountain, telling him that the Lord is merciful, gracious, slow to anger, and forgiving. God also adds, "yet by no means clearing the guilty, but visiting the iniquity of the parents upon the children and the children's children, to the third and the fourth genera-tion."[3] This statement seems strange and contradictory. Why would a loving, forgiving God punish children for something their parents did?

This Bible passage has spurred a lot of debate about generational sin—the idea that the sins of the parents can be passed on to the children. Some people may use these verses as an excuse to justify their behaviour. It's easy to blame others for our sin (especially when we do face the consequences of others' bad choices in our lives).

Embracing victimhood and staying trapped in the cycle is simpler than making the effort to break out of it.

The fact that sin has consequences, which will likely impact the people around you, should be obvious. Someone who has been abused as a child, like Olivia from *Fringe*, will face challenges that someone who wasn't abused won't have to deal with. Olivia becomes a different person from her parallel universe counterpart—more reserved, more empathetic, more afraid to love others— because of this abuse. Her struggles are a consequence of her stepfather's sin. But her stepfather's actions don't dictate her current behaviour. And they weren't God's judgement being heaped upon her.

Ezekiel 18 deals with this exact attitude. It seems that the Israelites had developed a proverb about the sins of their ancestors trapping them in the present—"The parents have eaten sour grapes, and the children's teeth are set on edge."[4] But God tells Ezekiel that the people can set aside this kind of thinking and affirms, over and over, that God judges the actions of individuals:

> "As I live, says the Lord God, this proverb shall no more be used by you in Israel. Know that all lives are mine; the life of the parent as well as the life of the child is mine: it is only the person who sins that shall die."[5]

In John, Jesus says the same thing to his disciples, who are caught up with the idea of generational sin. When they encounter a blind man, the disciples ask him, "Rabbi, who sinned, this man or his parents, that he was born blind?" Jesus replies, "Neither," and heals the man.[6] This story is powerful because Jesus frees these characters from their pasts—the disciples from believing that their ancestors' sins bind them and the man from his blindness—but still acknowledges that the past has power (the man's blindness still impacts who he is moving forward). I'm hesitant to describe the healing itself as "freeing" the blind man, because someone with a disability is just as free as the next person; the point of the story is not that he was healed but, rather, that his disability was not a punishment.

In the end, it is not others' actions that dictate our relationship with God; it is our choices.

We are not trapped by the sins of those who came before us, though they may certainly make our lives more difficult. Abuse, alcoholism, substance use, addiction—all these things, even if initiated by generations before us, can make our choices so much more difficult than they should be. But still, like Lee, we *can* choose who we will become. Neither Lee, nor God, says that decision will be an easy one. But the choice is there.

At the end of the episode, Lincoln has taken to heart what Lee told him. When chasing down a villain who feels trapped into doing something evil, Lincoln says, "You can keep waiting for somebody else to define you, to give you your place in the world, or you can decide that you're not just somebody's broken puppet anymore. Choose!"

Whatever choices we have made in the past, whatever choices others have made that affect us, we have a blank slate in front of us. Christ has set us free to make whatever choices we want, and he opens his arms to those who choose to follow him.

It is up to us. Choose.

Key Scripture

> "For freedom Christ has set us free."
> —Galatians 5:1

Study Questions

1. Imagine what a parallel version of you would look like if you had made vastly different choices in your life. Do you want to be more or less like that person?

2. Have you ever blamed your own bad behaviour on someone or something else—perhaps on a parent, an authority, or a situation you felt you had no control over? Why do you think positioning yourself as the victim in these situations comes naturally?

3. Do you feel trapped by a choice you, or someone else, made in the past? How can you embrace the freedom that Christ offers?

---

1. *Fringe.* "Brown Betty," season 2, episode 20. Directed by Seith Mann. Warner Bros., 2010.
2. *Fringe.* "Everything In Its Right Place," season 4, episode 17. Directed by David Moxness. Warner Bros., 2012.
3. Exodus 34:7.
4. Ezekiel 18.2.
5. Ezekiel 18:3–4.
6. John 9:2.

42

TALKING BACK TO THE TOTAL PERSPECTIVE VORTEX

BY EMMA SKRUMEDA

"The Universe, as has been observed before, is an unsettlingly big place, a fact which for the sake of a quiet life most people tend to ignore."
—*The Restaurant at the End of the Universe* by Douglas Adams[1]

Read: Judges 6–7

Reflect: Frogstar B is the most desolate planet in the universe. Nobody lives on its surface. Nothing grows in its soil. The world is home to a solitary piece of machinery—the Total Perspective Vortex, which is a torture device so brutal that it bears the reputation of being the only thing in any galaxy that can crush a person's soul. Its mechanism is remarkably simple: it shows you yourself. Yourself, to scale, in a rendered model of the entire universe. You are a "microscopic dot on a microscopic dot" within the cosmos. Anyone who enters the Total Perspective Vortex leaves with their mind totally and utterly destroyed, unable to withstand the knowledge of their own utter insignificance in the grand scheme of existence.

Everyone, except Zaphod Beeblebrox.

Zaphod, former President of the Galaxy rendered fugitive in *The Restaurant at the End of the Universe*, emerges from the Total Perspective Vortex unharmed, concerned only with getting something to eat. Due to a series of carefully orchestrated events, when Zaphod enters the Total Perspective Vortex, he is not in the real universe, but rather a synthesized one—a fake reality designed with him at the centre. This is what saves him for, in the Vortex, he is shown not the meaninglessness of his existence, but the importance of it.

In the book of Judges, when God tells Gideon that he is the one who will deliver the Israelites from their oppression under the nation of Midian, Gideon responds as a man who is very much aware of his own inconsequentiality:

> "...How can I save Israel? My clan is the weakest in Manasseh, and I am the least in my family."[2]

I am but a microscopic dot on a microscopic dot, he protests.

He is so concerned with his own weakness that he puts God through a series of tests. Gideon asks God for sign after sign to prove that he's been chosen to deliver Israel. First, he asks God to stay until he brings God a present; Gideon prepares a goat, unleavened cakes, and broth. An angel sets the food on fire, and Gideon realizes it really is God who is speaking to him. But even though Gideon knows God is speaking to him, he still wants more signs that God has chosen him to deliver Israel, so he tests God some more.

Gideon is terrified that he is too small to do what is being asked of him. He is focused on one limited perspective, convinced that he cannot do what God is asking. His insecurities are so great that they make him doubt not only himself, but God's ability to work through him.

When Gideon finally does respond to God's call, he arrives with a battalion at his back. God instructs Gideon to whittle down his troops, until, in the end, Gideon is sent against the Midianites with only 300 fighters behind him. Small as their forces are, the Israelites emerge victorious against their enemies, winning their nation a 40-year peace.

All this through a man who considered himself the least of his family.

It can be very daunting, recognizing one's own smallness. And it is easy for such acknowledgement to turn into apathy. "I am only one person," we tell ourselves. "There is nothing meaningful that I could accomplish." We become overwhelmed by feelings of our own powerlessness, by the size of our enemies, by our knowledge that we are but a microscopic dot on a microscopic dot when compared to the vastness of the universe.

But God has no such doubts of our worth. The One who created creation finds us in it, and loves us. God sees us as Zaphod sees himself in the Total Perspective Vortex —each of us is unfathomably precious and important, the very number of hairs on our heads accounted for.

It can be difficult to accept such a love, to believe that it's possible for every flaw to be seen, every mistake to be known, and to still be loved without reservation. We often do not extend such grace to ourselves, because we're our own worst critics. How to even begin unraveling the lies we've told ourselves, or that others have told us, the ones saying we are too small, too broken, too weak, and too insignificant to ever be able to accomplish anything?

Proverbs 3:5 reads: "Trust in the Lord with all your heart, and do not lean on your own understanding." That's where we begin: by trusting God. By being willing to let go of our own certainties and accept that we may be wrong in how we view ourselves. We take the first step towards re-establishing our value in Christ. It's hard, it's humbling, and it can leave us feeling vulnerable to cast aside a shell of "at least nobody can think less of me than I already do." But think of how amazing life could be if we see ourselves the way God does.

Having survived his encounter with the Total Perspective Vortex, Zaphod goes on to complete the mission he has spent years working towards, a task that only six others in the galaxy previously accomplished: he meets the man who rules the universe. Talk about a microscopic dot getting stuff done!

On the whole, Zaphod is self-absorbed, insensitive, and irresponsible. And no, we shouldn't emulate his personality (Gideon, as well, does not have an unblemished record and in later life leads Israel into idolatry).[3] But we could borrow just a pinch of Zaphod's reckless bravery, and dare to believe in our own significance. Not so that we become arrogant or egotistical, but so we become confident in our empowerment to work for good. Our reality is one where the Creator of the Universe loves us, values us *individually*, is with us, and promises to do good works through us. How's that for perspective?

Think of what we could accomplish if released from the narrative of being too small to achieve anything. Let's stop waiting for signs and testing God and instead do as we have been called to, taking action to change the world around us for the better.

Key Scripture

"Are not five sparrows sold for two pennies? And not one of them is forgotten before God. Why, even the hairs of your head are all numbered. Fear not; you are of more value than many sparrows."
—Luke 12:6–7

Study Questions

1. Gideon craves assurance that he is part of God's plan and is capable of doing great things in God's name. What encourages you to embrace your identity as a child of God?

2. Have you felt insignificant, like Gideon? Why?

3. What is a step you can take today, no matter how small, to work toward a God-inspired goal that you have been afraid to try achieving?

---

1. Adams, Douglas. *The Restaurant at the End of the Universe.* Pan Books, 1981.
2. Judges 5:15.
3. Judges 8:22–28.

ACKNOWLEDGEMENTS

Thank you to everyone who made this book possible, especially the writers who spent so much time working on their contributions and the editors who put it all together.

Thanks to all our beta readers: Aaron Thiessen, Anna Chemar, Daniel Bergman, Dennis Maione, Gordon Matties, Janet Hamm, Jordan Phillips, Julia Hamm, Lisa Wiebe, Lori Matties, Marvin Hamm, Mary Anne Isaak, Rachel Twigg, Seth Freeman, Shaneen Thompson, and Xw Webster.

Our appreciation goes out to Edreen Cielos (Paper Beats Rock) for the *incredible* artwork on the cover.

This book wouldn't exist without Mythos & Ink's patrons: Alex Mellen, Brian Gervais, Casey L. Covel, Charles S, ComrAdversaries, Dennis Maione, Elisabeth Wiebe, Glen, Jason Dueck, Jordan Phillips, Julia Hamm, Matt Civico, Mike Schroeder, Mitchell Wiebe, Naomi Strain, Ron Segstro, T.D. McIntosh, Victoria Grace Howell, Zach Schuster, and Zachary Sigurdson. You are all wonderful human beings.

Thanks to all you geeks for picking up this book and letting your faith be stretched by thinking deeply about popular media and how it can relate to God's word.

ABOUT THE WRITERS

Allison Alexander writes articles, edits sci-fi and fantasy books, and plays video games the rest of the time. She is the incurable author of *Super Sick: Making Peace with Chronic Illness*, an honest (and occasionally sarcastic) testimony about living with a chronic illness. Allison makes her home in Hoth, a.k.a. Winnipeg, Manitoba, with her husband and their imaginary pet dragon. Find her on aealexander.com.

Dan Bergman lives in Winnipeg, Manitoba, with his dear wife, and he teaches music to middle school students by day. By evening, night, and weekend, he teaches music to anyone via video game soundtracks on his podcast *Overtone Warpzone*, and teaches board games to anyone as part of the YouTube channel *Games Explained*. He really likes *Smash Bros.* (when he's not losing).

Nathan K. Campbell is a software engineer and the owner of far too many board games (if such a thing is possible). He enjoys reading and writing science fiction, fantasy, and theology. He lives in Texas with his wife, three children, and three too many dogs.

Matt Civico writes from Montreal, QC, where he and his wife do their best to prize food, cheer, and song above hoarded gold. He is the editor of *Common Pursuits*, co-host of *Stranger Still: A Stranger Things Podcast*, and he also writes the *Good Words* newsletter. Find him at mattcivico.com.

Kevin Cummings writes to sort out his thoughts about life, faith, and truth. His entry into fandom began with the original *Star Trek* series and has grown to include more films and franchises than he can count. He lives in Utah, is married, has two grown sons, and spends his days working for a technical college.

Jason Dueck's affection for science fiction and role-playing games comes as no surprise to anyone who's seen his Star Wars lunch box full of polyhedral dice. When he's not busy recounting the secrets hidden in the latest Marvel movie trailer, he works in non-profit communications.

Ellen Elliott is the author of *Geek and Ye Shall Find*, a devotional for Christian geeks and nerds.

Jonathan Elsensohn decided in seminary to follow in Jesus' footsteps and become a carpenter. He currently serves as the pastor of the First Baptist Church in Freehold, NJ, and he still enjoys woodworking. Before he became part of the clergy, he spent more hours than is reasonable playing clerics in D&D (2nd edition: THACO or bust!). He is married to the cutest, chicken-raising ninja.

James Felix is a graduate of Southwestern Assemblies of God University and has worked in Christian broadcasting for over 13 years. When not geeking out over Star Wars, Star Trek, and *The Lord of The Rings,* he can be found participating in medieval reenactment and cohosting the podcast *Geek at Arms.*

Victoria Grace Howell is an award-winning, multi-published author from Atlanta, Georgia, who enjoys writing essays, short stories, and novels. When she isn't typing furiously on her laptop, she's travelling, drinking tea, or snuggling with her white cat, Lessy.

Philippa Isom is a follower of Jesus, mother of two, and wife of one. Education Lecturer at Massey University in New Zealand, she loves glitter, unicorns, and anything shiny. She enjoys sci-fi with an A.I. bent.

Justin Koop is a father, husband, gamer, and music maker. Justin works as the Guild Master of Limit Break—a guild dedicated to providing a safe, inclusive, and friendly community where nerd and geek culture hobbies and culture can thrive.

Lester Liao is the Director of Common Pursuits and a pediatrician based in Toronto. He's written about video games for the *National Post* and more broadly for *CBC, The Globe and Mail,* and others.

Ashley Mowers is a scholar, playwright, and the Communications Director for Church of the Good Shepherd in Brentwood, TN. In 2019, she was made the Artist in Residence for the Institute of Theology, Imagination, and the Arts at the University of St. Andrews, where she developed original material for the stage. Ashley is a co-host on *The Min/Max Podcast*, where they discuss all things nerd culture and theology.

Michael Penner is a teacher everywhere he goes. With interests ranging from math and board games to sports and music, he is most passionate about helping people find joy in learning.

Kyle Rudge has over a decade of experience in journalism, broadcasting, and marketing. He's a geek through and through, a jungle main, a Ravenclaw, a devoted husband, the father of two humans, and the guardian of one furry companion. He derives joy from helping other creatives reach their full potential.

Charles Sadnick writes for *Beneath the Tangles*, the website he established to analyze the intersection of Christian faith and otaku culture. When he's not daydreaming about keeping peace in the galaxy through his Jedi training or conniving to take the Iron Throne, he works as an agency director and historian, and spends most of his free time with his wife and children playing video games and watching anime.

Dustin Schellenberg spends his time exploring the far reaches of space, understanding the ancient ways of might and magic, and wandering the post-apocalyptic wastes.

He sees God in all his fandoms and loves to share that revelation with the world through writing. He is father of two, husband of one, a sometimes theologian, and Free Methodist pastor in Winnipeg, Manitoba.

Jen Schlameuss is a mother of two teenage sons, a ninja, a raiser of chickens, and an avid consumer of all things superhero, science fiction, and fantasy. She is the author of *Comic Con Christianity* from Paulist Press. Jen is currently the pastoral associate of the Co-Cathedral of St. Robert Bellarmine in Freehold, New Jersey, and she is married to the cutest Baptist Pastor on the planet.

Jared and Nathan Siebert are a father/son duo from Saskatoon, SK. They love watching movies and TV together, often pausing to talk about a scene's composition or the plot's philosophical implications (you probably don't want to invite them to movie night). Jared researches and facilitates Canadian church planting efforts. Nathan is interested in pursuing a career in visual storytelling.

Emma Skrumeda is a writer, editor, and makeup artist. She loves lists, hates all things cherry-flavoured, and bears the reputation of cursed dice-roller. She lives in Winnipeg with her husband and their two cats in an apartment boasting more swords than rooms.

Aaron Thiessen wears a lot of different hats: husband, father, wannabe contemplative, amateur nerd, middling molecular mixologist, and pastor for youth and young adults at River East Church in Winnipeg, MB.

Shaneen Thompson lives in Alberta, Canada, with her husband and their far-too-sassy-for-his-own-good beagle. She writes about faith and geekery at *The Hoot & Howl*, binges on Marvel TV shows (and anything else with a great story), and likes to shoot fire at as many things as she can in TTRPGs.

Tim Webster is a husband and father of three. He and his wife have thoroughly inducted their family into geekdomhood. He is a fan of comics, superheroes, fantasy, and science fiction—particularly Star Trek and *Doctor Who*—but not as much Star Wars as you might expect for someone who teaches lightsaber combat.

Robert White remembers ignoring sermons warning about the dangers of reading and watching science fiction and fantasy as a teen. He's a journalist and author who specializes in the intersection of faith and culture. Geekdom favourites include C.S. Lewis and J.R.R. Tolkien, Star Trek and *The Expanse*. He lives in Guelph, Ontario, with his wife, Pam, and cat, Smokey.

Courtney Young is a wife, a mother, a pastor, a Gryffindor, a firebender, a Minnesotan, and a cat person. She has been diligently reading SFF since she could bike to the Circle Pines library on her own and just happened to check out a copy of Tamora Pierce's *Wild Magic*.

facebook.com/mythosandink

instagram.com/mythosandink

twitter.com/mythosandink

SO LONG AND THANKS FOR ALL THE REVIEWS!

Thanks for reading! If you enjoyed this book, please consider leaving an honest review on Goodreads and your favourite bookseller's website. These reviews are the second breakfasts to our hobbit hearts, the fish fingers in our custard, the clerics in our parties, the... well, you get the idea.

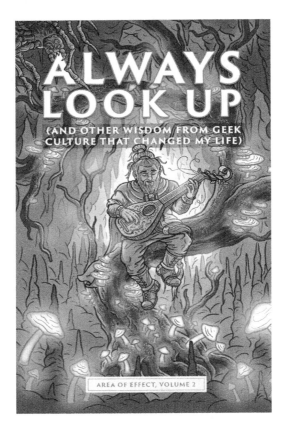

Always Look Up (and Other Wisdom from Geek Culture that Changed My Life) is a collection of essays on TV shows, movies, video games, and anime, exploring themes in pop culture with a critical, personal, and social justice-oriented lens.

JOIN A
SCI-FI AND FANTASY
COMMUNITY

DISCOVER
new and upcoming books to read.

MEET
other readers, writers, and bloggers.

DISCUSS
worldbuilding and writing.

LEARN
from editors and authors.

JOIN OUR DISCORD SERVER!

 MYTHOS & INK
www.mythosink.com/community

Made in the USA
Coppell, TX
29 April 2021